LIVING WITH PURPOSE BIBLE STUDY

Acts

LIVING WITH PURPOSE BIBLE STUDY

Acts

Guideposts

A Gift from Guideposts

Thank you for your purchase! We want to express our gratitude for your support with a special gift just for you.

Dive into ***Spirit Lifters***, a complimentary e-book that will fortify your faith, offering solace during challenging moments. Its 31 carefully selected scripture verses will soothe and uplift your soul.

Please use the QR code or go to **guideposts.org/spiritlifters** to download.

Living with Purpose Bible Study: Acts

Published by Guideposts
100 Reserve Road, Suite E200
Danbury, CT 06810
Guideposts.org

Cover design by Judy Ross
Interior design by Judy Ross
Cover photo by Vladimirovic/iStock
Typeset by Aptara, Inc.

ISBN 978-1-961442-81-8 (hardcover)
ISBN 978-1-961442-82-5 (softcover)
ISBN 978-1-961442-83-2 (ebook)

Printed and bound in the United States of America

CONTENTS

About Living with Purpose Bible Study

For as long as humankind has existed, we have pondered our place in the universe. Poets and preachers, philosophers and scientists alike have explored the topic for generations. Our busy modern lives leave little time for contemplation, and yet we move through our lives with nagging questions in the back of our minds: *Why am I here? What am I meant to do with my life?*

Fyodor Dostoevsky wrote that the "mystery of human existence lies not in just staying alive, but in finding something to live for." You might wonder how living with purpose ties in with the Bible. That's because God's Word is a guidebook for life, and God Himself has a purpose—a unique mission—for and unique to you. Reading the Bible and seeking God through prayer are two of the main ways God speaks to people. And when we begin to seek God, when we pursue His truth, when we begin to live our lives in ways that reflect His love back to others, we begin to find that purpose. Finding our purpose is not a destination; it is a journey we'll travel until we leave this earth behind and go to our heavenly Father.

Most of us know something about the Bible. We might be able to quote verses that we memorized as kids. Many of us have read parts of it, have learned about it in Sunday school both as children and adults. But not as many of us *know* the Bible, and that is where this Bible study comes in.

"Bible study" is a term that can elicit a variety of responses. For some people, the feeling that comes is a daunting sense of intimidation, even fear, because we worry that the Bible will somehow find us wanting, less than, rejected. Maybe we've heard preachers wielding the Bible as a weapon, using it as a measuring rod and a dividing line that separates "us" from "them."

Guideposts' *Living with Purpose Bible Study* addresses these questions and concerns with a hope-filled, welcoming, inclusive voice, like the one you've grown to know and love from Guideposts' devotional books, story collections, magazines, and website.

Best of all, you'll discover that the writers of *Living with Purpose Bible Study* are experts not only in the depth of their Bible knowledge but also in sharing that knowledge in such a welcoming, winning way that you can't help but be drawn in.

The writers come alongside you as trusted friends, guiding you through each volume in that warm, inviting manner that only Guideposts could bring you.

Each volume in the study draws from five trusted translations of the Bible: the New International Version, New American Standard Bible, the Amplified Version, the English Standard Version, and the King James Version of the Bible. We encourage you to keep your favorite Bible translation on hand as you read each study chapter. The Bible passages you read act as the foundation from which the study writer's insights, information, and inspiration flow. You can read along with the writers as each chapter unfolds, or you can read all of the passages or verses included in the chapter prior to reading it. It's up to you; you can use the method that works best for you.

In addition, you'll find two distinct features to enhance your experience: "A Closer Look" entries bring context by presenting historical, geographical, or cultural information, and "Inspiration from Acts" entries demonstrate the spiritual insights people like you have gained from their knowledge of the biblical text. We've also provided lined writing spaces at the end of each lesson for you to jot down your own thoughts, questions, discoveries, and *aha* moments that happen as you read and study.

A final note: Before you read each chapter, we encourage you to pray, asking that God will open your eyes and heart to what He has to say. Our prayer for you is that you find a new or renewed sense of purpose and grow closer to God as you deepen your understanding of God's Word by enjoying this *Living with Purpose Bible Study*.

—The Editors of Guideposts

An Overview of Acts

Reading the book of Acts is like watching an epic motion picture, an adventure story that begins in Jerusalem and culminates some thirty years and thousands of miles later in Rome, the capital of a vast empire that stretched from Britain to Arabia.

The characters in this drama include names both familiar and obscure, as well as important characters who remain unnamed. You'll meet provincial governors and kings, soldiers and centurions, common folk and aristocrats. There is Stephen, the first Christian to die for his faith; a traveling Ethiopian finance officer, puzzled by the book of Isaiah; James, the Lord's brother and head of the Jerusalem church; Cornelius, a God-fearing Roman to whom an angel appeared in a dream; Early Church "power couple" Aquila and Priscilla; a prosperous businesswoman named Lydia; and pioneering co-missionaries with Paul, Silas and Barnabas—an almost endless cast of vivid characters. As the story opens, Simon Peter is the main character, while the spotlight falls on Paul during the last part. However, throughout the entire story, the central figure is always Jesus, the risen Lord.

The book of Acts gives us our only record of the beginnings of Christianity—from Jesus's instructions to His disciples between the resurrection and His ascension, to the coming of the Holy Spirit at Pentecost and the founding of God's new order, the church. From Jerusalem, empowered believers took the Good News of salvation throughout Judea, Samaria, and Galilee—all of Palestine. And from there we trace its rapid-fire spread to Syrian Antioch, Asia Minor, Greece, and finally to Rome.

As with most books of the Bible, scholars offer different theories for its authorship but do not suggest a definitive or clear alternative to Luke the physician. As evidence, they point to accounts or doctrines that differ between Acts and the Pauline Epistles (the letters Paul wrote to the Early Church congregations), such as accounts of Paul's conversion and first contacts with the leaders of the fledgling church.

But traditionally and historically, Luke has been accepted as the author of Acts, and there is still wide acceptance of his authorship today. This authorship gives Luke, the only Gentile writer in the New Testament, the distinction of writing more than one-fourth—around 27 percent—of the New Testament. We are not sure of Luke's beginnings, but tradition suggests that he may have come from either Syrian Antioch or Philippi. We do know that he was a physician, a companion of Paul in many of his travels, and an able writer and historian.

The book of Acts tells us that Luke was with Paul on his last trip to Jerusalem, throughout his imprisonment at Caesarea, and on his final journey to Rome. This means that much of Acts is an eyewitness account, and the parts that are not firsthand came to Luke from reliable eyewitnesses.

The time and place in which Acts was written cannot be determined for certain. However, tradition—history passed down through many generations—seems to favor a date between AD 60 and 70. Although there are those who would date the writing as late as the early part of the second century, it is generally conceded that it would not have appeared later than AD 90. Tradition also holds that it was written in Rome.

Continuing with the movie metaphor, the book of Acts, also known as the Acts of the Apostles, is a sequel to the Gospel of Luke. Writing under the inspiration of the Holy Spirit, Luke continues the story that begins in his Gospel, and in his second volume he shows us what happened to the Christian faith after Jesus's ascension.

The time covered by the book of Acts spans approximately AD 29–67. This was a time of peace and stability in the Roman Empire. Travel was relatively easy and safe. The common language of Greek made communication possible throughout the empire. In short, the stage was set and the time was ripe for the expansion of the Christian community. And that is precisely what the book of Acts describes in a fast-paced narrative that rivals the best Hollywood screenplay.

But we should not let the fast-moving quality of the book blind us to the careful piece of history that it is. Luke demonstrates the same care for order and detail in this book that he did in his earlier Gospel account. Many scholars agree that the foundation of the book can be found in Acts 1:8. Here we see both the centrality of the Holy Spirit and the plan of expansion that can be traced throughout the rest of the book: "You will be my witnesses in Jerusalem, and in all Judea and Samaria, and to the ends of the earth" (Acts 1:8, NIV).

Thematically, Acts focuses on the work of the Holy Spirit in and through the lives of the early disciples. In fact, some scholars have suggested that the book could have been titled

"The Acts of the Holy Spirit through the Apostles." As we study this book, we will often focus on the idea of effective witnessing, drawing parallels between the first century and ours. In addition, we will come in contact with the basic content of early Christianity through a number of important sermons. And from start to finish we will see how God worked to create Christian community and to establish Christianity as a worldwide religion.

A knowledge of the message of Acts is essential if we are to understand how Christianity moved from Jesus to Paul—from Palestine to the world. Without it we would not only have a historical "blank," but we would also fail to discover many ways in which the Holy Spirit can use us in the continued sharing of the Good News and growth of the church.

As we move now into this important book that bridges the Gospels and the epistles, we find God at work through His Holy Spirit in the hearts of Jew and Gentile alike. We see a vigorous and energized young church on the move. The mood is one of holy restlessness as first-generation Christians witness the life-changing power of the gospel of Jesus.

The sweeping, cinematic stories that fill the book of Acts await us, so gather your favorite Bible or Bibles, pour yourself a nice cup of coffee or tea, and retreat to your favorite quiet place as we begin our study together.

LESSON 1: ACTS 1:1–2:4

Getting Ready to Go

Thank You for the privilege of learning more about witnessing to my faith through this lesson. Amen.

The book of Acts opens with a group of people whom God intended to use to change the world. But they were not ready yet. They didn't fully realize it, but they needed to be prepared. That's what the fifty days between the resurrection of Jesus and Pentecost were all about. It is easy for us to overlook this needed time of preparation because we are told so little about what happened during those days.

We are told, though, that during the forty days between His resurrection and His ascension, Jesus spoke to His disciples "about the kingdom of God" (1:3, ESV). This must have been the most intensive time of instruction the disciples had ever known. In his Gospel, Luke says that Jesus opened "their understanding, that they might understand the scriptures" (24:45, KJV). That in itself is amazing, and it speaks of the depth of teaching and learning that took place.

The Main Ingredients of Effective Witnessing (1:1–2)

Luke wastes no time in getting to the heart of what much of this book is about, which is Christian witnessing. In the first two verses we encounter the main ingredients of effective witnessing: the seeker, the servant, and the Savior. Because they are so important, we will look carefully at each of them right at the beginning. These three elements appear repeatedly throughout the book, and an examination of them will help us gain insights into our own witnessing today.

The Seeker

Theophilus, the person to whom Luke addressed both his Gospel and the book of Acts, is the seeker. The only clue we get about his relationship to Christianity is found in Luke 1:4, where he is said to have been "instructed" in the faith. This may mean he was a recent convert who was receiving initial training, or it may simply mean that Theophilus had been told some things about the faith and was still trying to make up his mind. Either way, though, he was interested enough to receive two lengthy communications from Luke.

We know little about Theophilus, whom Paul greets as the recipient of his account. His name may provide a clue. It means "one who loves God." Bible scholars have suggested that he could be a Jew from Alexandria, a Roman official, or even Paul's attorney—or that the name was a title, perhaps used to represent all who love God. One of the important messages of the book of Acts is that God puts "Theophiluses" (lovers of God) in our pathway. They may be outside or inside the church. Our challenge and opportunity is to be sensitive to them and to be willing to give them the time and attention they need to become enriched and whole in the Christian faith.

Even today many people outside the church are searching for God. They are sending loud signals by their involvement in cults and the occult, or in the rise of what pollsters call the "nones"—those who are not affiliated with any religion or faith but in many cases see themselves as spiritual. We see it in their growing despair over the world's problems and our inability to solve them. We also see it in their expressed feelings of alienation, distrust, and anxiety and by their often-failed attempts to find genuine relationships in the depersonalized world of social media. These are all signs that people are open to a relationship with God through Christ, and it is important for us to be sensitive to the "signals" that people around us today are sending.

Then there are Theophiluses within the church fellowship who have a marginal or cursory understanding of and commitment to the Christian faith. You might well know people like this, people who just might come alive if they were given special instruction, care, and attention from other believers.

The Servants

That's where the servants come into the picture. For every Theophilus, there must be at least one Luke. People are won by people. God reached us by becoming human in Jesus Christ. And we reach others by offering them our faith wrapped in our humanity. Christian witnessing is always "incarnational." It began with *the* Incarnation; it continues in the multiplied incarnations of Christ, who lives out His life through those who serve Him.

Who are the servants? The book of Acts supplies the answer. They are the quiet people—the servant Christians—most of whose names are not even recorded in Scripture. To be sure, there are some major figures and leaders in the drama of Acts, but these are outnumbered a thousand to one by the ordinary followers. The word *celebrity* doesn't exist in God's dictionary, but the word *saint* does. We must forever erase from our minds the notion that only the famous, the champions, and the beautiful are useful to God. This is often the erroneous impression we get in many media ministries. But it is just as false as the pre-Reformation belief that only the priests could rightly read and interpret the Bible. If we fall for the heresy of the "celebrity syndrome," it will take another Christian Reformation to set us right again.

The Savior

This brings us to the third ingredient, the Savior. The only reason we even dare to believe we can influence someone else's life for Christ is because Jesus is real and alive! He continued His ministry through the Holy Spirit after His ascension. Luke's first treatise was only what "Jesus began to do and teach." That's why a second volume was needed. But we must also remember that Christ's ministry did not end with the last page of Acts. It continues today.

There are more Theophiluses in the world right now than there were when Christ lived on the earth. And there are more Christians alive now than there were when Luke wrote Acts. When we couple that with the knowledge that Christ is just as alive as He ever was, we can know beyond a doubt that our

Christian witnessing is meant to be effective. The first two verses of Acts not only remind us of the main ingredients needed then, but they also place us squarely in the picture when it comes to sharing the gospel today. Our study of these lessons will be profitable as long as we keep that perspective clearly in mind.

The Master Teacher (1:3–11)

The ultimate purpose of teaching is not just to convey information but to change people. We've already said that the disciples needed to be changed, to be better prepared for the ministry that would soon be theirs. In Acts 1:3–11, Luke shows us Jesus's teaching method for accomplishing that change. And it is clear from the rest of Acts that the method was successful. The days between Jesus's resurrection and Pentecost was a time when the Master Teacher got His followers ready for the greatest challenge of their lives. Let's see how He did it.

Jesus Teaches by Revelation

He concentrated first on *revelation.* Luke says that "He also presented Himself alive after His suffering, by many convincing proofs" (1:3, NASB). The Greek language used here is quite strong, with each modifying word in "many infallible proofs" reinforcing the others. If we were saying it today, we might put it this way: "Jesus showed Himself alive in ways that left *no doubt about it.*" This was precisely what the disciples needed. They had to *know* that death had not defeated Jesus. It would never have been enough to be told this. They had to see and experience it.

The old saying is correct: "Seeing *is* believing." Jesus knew that, so He showed Himself alive (1:3) in ways that couldn't be questioned. And the exclamation "We have seen Him!" became the foundation upon which Christianity was built. Even today we must continue to "see" Christ through the witness of Scripture and 2,000 years of testimony by those who have been changed by Him. And we continue to see Him through our own inner witness and personal experience—saying along with the saints of the ages, "He touched me!" That revelation and our experience of (and witness to) it are still central in the Christian faith.

Jesus Teaches by Providing Instruction

But Jesus did not stop there. Luke next tells us that He provided *instruction*. During those forty days, Jesus was "speaking of the things pertaining to the kingdom of God" (1:3, KJV). Confidence needed to be linked with content. Experience needed to be enriched with information. This is at least one reason why Luke was inspired to record the content of several sermons delivered by early Christian leaders (such as those in chapters 7, 10, 13, and 25). Christianity not only warms the heart but also enlightens the mind. It has substance as well as emotion. And the two work together to create reality.

Luke does not go into detail about the instruction. He simply says that the focal point was the Kingdom of God. Linking this with what we know of the Kingdom from biblical teaching, this seems to mean that Jesus wanted to drive home the point that in His coming, a new order or fellowship had begun. This was easier to know and experience as long as He was physically present, but the disciples had to know it as truth even in His physical absence. They had to understand that in Christ, God had split history down the middle. From now on everything was to be interpreted in light of Christ's coming. Now the mission of the disciples was to be that of proclaiming, interpreting, and expanding the Kingdom—that is, helping others come to the place of seeing, experiencing, and living life from that perspective too.

As the events in the book of Acts unfold, we see this perspective working itself out in the disciples' witnessing and preaching. In Greek, this is the *kerygma*—meaning the "proclamation" of the Early Church. Because we will be reading and studying several sermons in Acts, let's review what the basic elements of the kerygma were so we will recognize them in our study:

1. The coming of Jesus fulfills Old Testament prophecy.
2. Jesus is the Messiah and proclaims the Kingdom of God.
3. The fact of Jesus's resurrection is the main proof of Christianity's truthfulness.
4. Jesus will one day return to establish the Kingdom on earth.
5. The only way to participate in the Kingdom (for time and eternity) is to believe in Jesus as the Savior.

It's exciting to visualize the disciples meeting daily with Jesus during the forty days between His resurrection and ascension and filling their minds with these truths until their hearts burned to share the Good News with others. Who of us would not have a message to share if the Lord Himself were to teach us in person for forty days as He did the disciples!

One important point to remember is that the Christian message is not something *we* invent. It is something Christ gives. At the end of this forty-day period, the disciples knew *what* they were to share. They didn't have to devise or invent a message; they had only to report it. And the rest of the book of Acts confirms that they did this conscientiously, qualitatively, and enthusiastically. As the Early Church began to grow, instruction was an all-important function: "And they continued stedfastly in the apostles' doctrine and fellowship" (2:42, KJV), and "Day after day, in the temple courts and from house to house, they never stopped teaching and proclaiming the good news that Jesus is the Messiah" (5:42, NIV).

Unfortunately, this same spirit doesn't always prevail today. Without serious Bible study, many in the church are still "infants" in their knowledge of and ability to share the Christian faith. While many people claim to have had some kind of "experience" with Christ, they can easily become walking proof that subjective experience alone is insufficient. Experience without instruction is shallow enthusiasm and not to be trusted. Instruction without experience is dead intellectualism. The early Christians taught us that to have vitality and life in our faith, instruction and experience must go together.

Jesus Teaches on Sharing the Good News

But still, there is more to Jesus's method. There is *impartation*: "and you will be my witnesses," He said (1:8, ESV). Early on, the disciples knew they were to be commissioned to carry on Christ's work. Jesus was appealing to that part of the human personality that responds positively to being involved and needed. Studies in business and industry have shown that worker productivity and efficiency increase when employees feel they are consulted and appreciated. The same is true in the fellowship of faith—the church. As people are actively involved in witnessing and working for the Lord in ministering to physical and spiritual needs, the church comes alive and experiences vitality. There is no such thing as a spectator Christian. We are all called to be participants—team players—in living and sharing the Good News of Jesus Christ.

Jesus's Teaching and Acting the Good News

Behind Jesus's method is the idea that every Christian is intended to be a *functioning* member of the body of Christ. The category of "inactive member" is really a misnomer. In truth there's only one kind of authentic church member: active and involved. To be a disciple of Christ is to hear the call and respond with action.

But surely the feeling of anticipation and excitement did not last long before the disciples asked themselves, "How in the world are we ever going to be able to do it?" They knew they couldn't duplicate Jesus's work under their own power. But in response, Jesus promised that His method of impartation also included the indispensable factor, the Holy Spirit: "You will receive power when the Holy Spirit has come upon you" (1:8, NASB). In promising them the Spirit, Jesus was offering them the same presence and power that enabled Him to do His work.

We must not get the idea that Jesus accomplished His earthly mission on earth in the flesh. Earlier, Luke had made it plain that Jesus did His work "in the power of the Spirit" (Luke 4:14, KJV; see also 4:18). And in Jesus's final instructions to His disciples, He made it clear that they would succeed only by the power of the Spirit: "Stay in the city until you have been clothed with power from on high" (Luke 24:49, NIV), and "wait for the gift my Father promised" (Acts 1:4, NIV).

It is important that we properly understand what Jesus meant here in relation to our own discipleship. So often the words *stay* and *wait* have been misinterpreted as a call to passivism. Well-meaning people have sometimes said, "We must not do anything unless we have received the Spirit." But we are living on this side of Pentecost. The Spirit has been given! We don't have to wait for Him to come. He has come and is here.

At the same time, though, we must not be deluded into thinking that all of the pronouncements and actions of Christians and the church are automatically done "in the Spirit." The pages of history are dotted with tragic stories of people who acted erroneously—at times even perpetrating atrocious cruelties—while claiming to be doing it "in the Spirit." We cannot maintain and expand the ministry of Christ and the church by operating on a blank-check principle that assumes God automatically agrees with decisions simply because a group of Christians made them.

How, then, shall we steer the proper course between these two errors? The answer comes in recognizing that on the day of Pentecost, God dug the well of the Spirit for Christians and the church in all time. We do not have to wait for a replay of Pentecost. But like the first disciples, we must drink from the well. That is, we must act *after* we have interacted with the Spirit in contemplation and prayer. This is the kind of impartation Jesus gave His disciples: involvement mixed with dependence, happiness linked with humility, participation infused with power.

Jesus's Teaching on Correction

This part of our lesson also shows that our perspective is gained by another of Jesus's methods: *correction.* Verses 6 and 7 of chapter 1 show that Jesus had to correct a misunderstanding about the Kingdom. Despite the fact that the disciples had been receiving regular and deep instruction about the Kingdom of God, they were still filtering Jesus's words through a Jewish mindset. For over 400 years the Jews had longed for the coming of the Messiah. But they were convinced that His coming would mean the national and political restoration of the Davidic kingdom to Israel. So their question in verse 6—"Lord, are you at this time going to restore the kingdom to Israel?" (NIV)—while off base, is not unusual.

From our perspective we find it hard to understand that after being with Jesus for over three years, after witnessing His death and resurrection, they would still be so blind as to ask such a question. But with infinite patience, Jesus tries to help them see that the Kingdom of God takes priority over the kingdom of Israel. They had to understand that building the earthly kingdom is not the same as building the heavenly one. But above all, they had to know that *the* Kingdom of God is always bigger than our "lesser kingdoms." God's work is always bigger than our understanding of it.

Does this mean that we should abandon our "lesser kingdoms," the personal preferences and priorities that seem important to us? In many cases, no. More than likely the apostles continued to pray, as previous generations had, for the deliverance of Jerusalem and the restoration of the Davidic kingdom. But what changed was that they no longer saw the lesser kingdom as the ultimate priority or the only way God could work to accomplish His purposes. We learn from this that it is perfectly all right to hold to our perspective and priorities, but we must not be so arrogant as to limit the Kingdom of God to our view of it.

Jesus's Teaching on Assurance

Our lesson gives us one more element in Jesus's method: *assurance.* Assurance that they would never labor alone in their task (1:9–11). Even as Jesus's ascension was running its course, angels appeared to assure the disciples that He would "come in the same way as you saw him go into heaven" (1:11, ESV). And we have the complete picture when we couple this with His last promise: "I am with you always, to the end of the age" (Matthew 28:20, NASB).

Why was this assurance so important to the disciples? Simply because they had to "lose Jesus" again. They had lost Him the first time when He died on the cross. Now they were losing Him as He ascended into heaven and returned to His Father. But there is a difference. They walked down the hill of Calvary alone and lonely. But this time, when they walked down the hill called Olivet, the disciples were alone but not lonely! Even though they would never again walk with Christ in the flesh, they would never again be without the presence of His Spirit.

In a way these forty days with Jesus after His resurrection was the disciples' "senior year" of training before they were sent out on their own. But as with any graduation, it was only the commencement. They would be learners for the rest of their lives. And that learning process was to take on special significance as they left the mount of ascension and returned to their vigil in the upper room in Jerusalem.

Attending to Business (1:12–26)

For forty days the disciples had been with Jesus in some of the most important, intensive, and intimate times they had ever known. It would have been easy, even understandable, for them to have returned to Jerusalem to merely bask in the warm memories that their time with the Lord had produced. But they didn't. Instead, they attended to several strategic activities that made possible their readiness for the coming of the Spirit.

A Fellowship of Prayer

First of all, they "were continually devoting themselves with one mind to prayer" (1:14, NASB). This implies that the days between the ascension and Pentecost were lived in the atmosphere of prayer. Or to put it another way, the disciples continued (on another level) the communion with Christ that they had experienced during the preceding forty days. This was especially important, because not to have done so would have easily produced the feeling that they were living in a vacuum. Doubts could have begun to creep in. But through prayer, they stayed connected with the vision and the promise that Jesus had given them.

In C. S. Lewis's masterpiece *The Screwtape Letters*, he describes the senior devil—Screwtape—writing to the junior devil—Wormwood—about how to lead a new convert astray. Screwtape insists that the way to defeat the best efforts of a fledgling convert is to prevent him from feeling the need to pray. And then Screwtape adds that if that doesn't work, Wormwood is to get the convert to concentrate attention on himself rather than on Jesus. Had the disciples turned their gaze from Christ to themselves during those days of waiting, they could have easily fallen prey to discouragement or impatience. By focusing all their attention on Jesus, they were content to wait for the promise they knew was coming.

The Fellowship Restored to Full Strength

But we notice that the disciples didn't limit themselves to prayer. They also attended to a very practical matter (1:15–26). Here we see how the disciples dealt with the "gap" in their fellowship that resulted with the demise of Judas. The eleven disciples apparently felt the need to be at full strength in terms of leadership when the Spirit came. From this action we learn two important things about these early Christians, qualities that will serve us well in our own pilgrimage of faith.

First, the 120 or so individuals who were clustered together in the upper room were not "so heavenly minded that they were no earthly good," as the popular expression goes. Even though they were devoted to prayer, they were not "lost in prayer"—they didn't have their heads in the clouds. This is important because true discipleship is not measured by how "otherworldly" we are. Inattentiveness to practical matters is no mark of spirituality. Even the task of choosing next year's leaders is part of faithful discipleship. And on a mundane level, sometimes the most spiritual thing we can do is change a diaper, write a letter, or just take the time to listen—especially take the time to listen!

Brother Lawrence, the seventeenth-century monk who gave us the classic book *The Practice of the Presence of God*, reinforced this truth by showing us how he finally came to the place in his life where washing dishes in the monastery kitchen was just as much an act of devotion to God as was attending Communion in the monastery chapel. One of our greatest needs is to tear down the human-imposed barriers that separate the sacred from the secular. For the Christian, all of life is sacred.

In this act of selecting Judas's successor, we also see the disciples' concern for excellence of leadership. The only individuals considered were those who had demonstrated their faithfulness from the beginning (1:22). With these qualifications set forth, only two candidates emerged. And interestingly, they were two "quiet people." Neither Joseph, called Barsabas, nor Matthias is ever mentioned before or after this event. Although they were both considered appointable to this great task, by a casting of lots Matthias was selected (1:26).

We learn from this story that the best leaders may not be among those who are most prominent or among those who campaign hardest for the job. True leadership is something we rise to by demonstrating faithfulness and obedience; it isn't something we are given because of charisma or clout.

A United Fellowship

In reflecting on this part of our lesson, it is important to note that the disciples did all these things in close proximity to one another (1:13 and 2:1). This doesn't mean they were never separated from one another during these ten days. It does mean, though, that they recognized their need for one another, and it is likely they were together much of the time. But their unity was not simply one of physical location; it was also of spiritual oneness.

Their being "with one accord" (1:14, KJV) closely parallels Ezekiel's vision of the dry bones (Ezekiel 37:1–14). In this vivid picture we see that the next-to-the-last-stage of renewal was the coming together of the bones, complete with sinews and flesh. All that was missing was the breath of the Spirit of God. And when the breath of God came, "they lived, and stood up upon their feet" (Ezekiel 37:10, KJV).

We can picture this among the early Christians. Their time with Jesus and with each other had brought them together and had clothed them with the essentials. Only the Spirit was missing. And God graciously provided Him.

The True Beginning

This part of our lesson ends with the true beginning—the beginning of the new fellowship of believers, the church as God intended it to be (2:1–4). Even though Pentecost was ushered in with the most dramatic of manifestations (wind and tongues of fire), the more profound point must not be lost in the symbolism. Pentecost was God's inbreathing—"all of them were filled with the Holy Spirit" (2:4, NIV)—which enabled them to minister. Without the infilling of the Holy Spirit, nothing else would have really mattered. But with the coming of the Spirit, the church, like the collection of dry bones in the Ezekiel story, was enabled to march as a mighty and powerful army in the world. And those first-century Christians marched! As we shall see now in our ongoing study, within a few years their gospel of Good News had infiltrated the known world of that time.

These opening verses of Acts give us a vivid picture of the disciples' preparation time. Without those days of preparation on their part, we might not have been recipients of the gospel in our time.

The parallel between then and now is clear. We have here our model for action and for the future in this vignette of the "120" in the upper room who, through prayer, fellowship with one another, and empowerment by the Holy Spirit, were prepared to confront the future.

Lord Jesus, thank You for my times of fellowship with You, and thank You for the gift of the Holy Spirit. Help me always be attentive to His leading. Amen.

INSPIRATION FROM THE BOOK OF ACTS

But you will receive power when the Holy Spirit comes on you; and you will be my witnesses in Jerusalem, and in all Judea and Samaria, and to the ends of the earth.

—Acts 1:8, NIV

As a young Christian, I learned about Jesus's call to be His witness to the ends of the earth. I assumed I was meant to become a missionary. I read biographies of missionaries to faraway countries. I attended conferences and listened to talks by those serving on the other side of the globe. When Jesus didn't lead me in that direction, I felt as if I'd failed Him.

But Jesus is full of surprises. Through my choreography work, He provided me an opportunity to help a mission group in Hong Kong. In my writing life, He opened doors for my books to be translated into Dutch and Indonesian, and for my devotionals to reach around the world. I'm so grateful for those unexpected experiences to share my faith and the Good News of Jesus.

Serving on short-term mission trips and writing books aren't the only ways to be His witness far from home. In this age of the Internet, a post on social media can encourage others to praise Him. A letter can remind a friend far away to keep trusting Jesus. And most powerful of all, my prayers can join with those of missionaries who are serving at the ends of the earth. Just like the disciples, I am part of His kingdom, testifying to His love and grace, whether with my family and neighborhood or the far reaches of the planet.

—Sharon Hinck

Notes

Notes

LESSON 2: ACTS 2:5–8:3

Growing under Pressure

Heavenly Father, may I apply this lesson from Your Word to my heart and my actions. Thank You for giving me opportunities to grow in You. AMEN.

It would be difficult to find a term that more adequately describes the state of many people in our modern society than the word *stressed*. Stress has been called the epidemic of the twenty-first century. It's clear that we are a people under pressure. Almost daily, the medical world publishes new evidence for the negative effects of stress upon the mind and body. The publishing world continues to produce books on how to cope with stress. Even the church is discovering that burnout is real and counterproductive to true spirituality, among both laypeople and clergy, with blog entries and web articles dealing specifically with church-related stress and burnout.

Although they didn't use the same terms as we do, the early Christians knew what it was like to live their faith under stress. In this lesson we will examine some of the pressures they faced and see how they continued to minister and grow in spite of them.

Opportunity Unlimited (2:5–47)

A Unique Opportunity

Ironically, the first pressure the early Christians faced was the *pressure of opportunity* (2:5–47). We find that God timed the coming of the Holy Spirit with the Jewish celebration of Pentecost. No day, including the Passover, brought more people from all over the world than did the Day of Pentecost (2:5, 9–11). For the Jews it was a time to dedicate the firstfruits of their crops to God. For the Christians it became the "firstfruits" of a new wave of Christian believers who would, in time, grow throughout the world.

Nowadays, we have what might be called an excess of opportunity. Business owners and employees labor under the pressure of opportunity: meeting budgets and quotas, striving for increased sales or productivity goals, doing ever more with less and with fewer people, and so on. Although opportunities present us with a good time to demonstrate our abilities, they can also bring high anxiety. The tragedies and implications of failure continually hover over the situation. While the first Christians were not given any daily quotas to meet, they surely recognized the opportunity they had for "reaching the world" in the microcosm of people who were in Jerusalem that day of Pentecost.

Those first Christians wasted no time in *connecting* with the people. The coming of the Spirit supernaturally enabled them to share the gospel in many languages (2:4). Luke tells us that the people who jammed the streets of Jerusalem were from "every nation under heaven," and they were amazed that "each one heard their own language being spoken" (2:5–6, NIV). Something very strange was happening as that handful of Galileans witnessed to the "mighty works of God" (verse 11, ESV) with boldness and in a variety of languages.

Even if we're unable to "speak with other tongues" as the first disciples did, we will do well to realize the importance of "speaking the language" others can understand. For us today this will mean taking the time to establish credibility. People are skeptical of hype and the fast come-on. We have much better chances for success in sharing our Christian faith when we do so with compassion and a caring heart, and in a common language that everyone can readily understand.

The First Christian Sermon

We also learn from our Scripture lesson that after *connection* had been made with the crowd, *content* was given through the preaching of the first Christian sermon (2:14–36). Be sure to read carefully these twenty-three verses that make up the sermon as Luke has given it to us while we study and reflect on this lesson. Here again we see that vital and necessary connection between experience and information. For the folks present at this first sermon, it was understood that if they were expected to make an intelligent response to it, they must first of all *hear* it.

A good illustration of this is seen in the long and effective ministry of Lord Donald Soper (1903–1998), who witnessed for Christ each week in London's Hyde Park at the famous "speakers' corner." Lord Soper learned by experience that most of his listeners neither knew nor remembered the gospel story, and that if they were expected to make an intelligent response to it, they must first of all *hear* it.

On the Day of Pentecost, the focal point of this part of our lesson, that *hearing* came through Peter's sermon. For in this sermon we have a superb model of *kerygma*, one of the four styles of preaching that was prevalent in the Early Church. Here is a bold proclamation of the truth of the gospel.

It is also significant that this first Christian sermon was delivered by Peter. What a fantastic study in contrasts! Less than two months earlier Peter had turned coward in front of just a few people in the courtyard of the high priest and denied that he was one of Jesus's disciples. But now this same Peter, loved and forgiven by his resurrected Lord and empowered by the Holy Spirit, stood boldly before the masses in Jerusalem and proclaimed that Jesus of Nazareth was indeed the Messiah.

It should also be noted that this sermon is a masterpiece of argument. Because of the joy expressed by the Spirit-filled disciples, their critics accused them of being drunk. But in the beginning of his sermon, Peter refutes this by reminding them that it was only nine o'clock in the morning, and then he tells the crowd that what they are seeing is a fulfillment of Joel's prophecy: "I will pour out my Spirit on all people. Your sons and daughters will prophesy, your old men will dream dreams, your young men will see visions" (Joel 2:28, NIV).

We can be sure that Peter's opening words had the attention of the crowd, and from that point on he opened up the Scriptures to prove that Jesus Christ was the fulfillment of the Messianic words of the prophets and that His coming fulfilled their predictions. And then Peter came to his grand climax with the words, "Let all the house of Israel therefore know for certain that God has made him both Lord and Christ, this Jesus whom you crucified" (2:36, ESV).

For Luke, here is the clear confirmation of Jesus's words in Acts 1:8. Peter's sermon is a ringing call to the universal proclamation and evangelization that dominates the story in the rest of the book of Acts. Since Luke himself does not personally enter the scene until Acts 16:10, it seems entirely possible that he was a convert to the same kind of message that Peter preached on the Day of Pentecost. His writing is not a dispassionate reporting of historical events; rather, it is the record of one who had himself been transformed by the gospel message.

The Crowd's Response

Luke now tells us that Peter's message spoke to their hearts and moved them to *conviction*—to a sense of guilt and a recognition of need (2:37–40). Luke's words paint a graphic picture: "Now when they heard this, they were cut to the heart [with remorse and anxiety], and they said to Peter and the rest of the apostles, 'Brothers, what are we to do?'" (2:37, AMP). This was an expression of genuine conviction born out of a dramatic encounter with the Word of God. We see no sign of manipulation here on Peter's part. There is no playing on the emotions of the crowd. Yet Peter and the rest of the disciples knew that the point of their message announcing the Good News was to call for a response. And as Peter preached, we see him moving closer and closer to the place where those who heard him would have to respond.

Notice that Peter's answer to their question was couched in the atmosphere of repentance: "Repent, and each of you be baptized in the name of Jesus Christ for the forgiveness of your sins" (2:38, NASB). Repentance is fundamental. The gospel demands repentance, that is, a turning away from sin. True repentance involves a change of both heart and action. When repentance is coupled with baptism (i.e., the rite that signifies entry into a new way of life), the responders can demonstrate and model the complete "turning" that is implied in the term *conversion.* And it was this that Peter called for at the end of his sermon.

We cannot truly receive Christ until we have first confessed and turned our back on (repented of) the sin in our lives. It can be argued that one of the major weaknesses in modern-day Christianity is its attempt to operate on the assumption that you can "have Christ" without making fundamental changes in belief systems, behaviors, habits, and so forth. The first-century Christians made no such assumption.

Next, Luke tells us that those who responded were wholeheartedly welcomed into the *community* (2:41–47). The disciples knew that without immediate and sustained nurturing, their new converts would not hold steady in their faith. Verse 42 tells us exactly what they did to encourage growth and faithfulness: "And they devoted themselves to the apostles' *teaching* and the *fellowship*, to the *breaking of bread* and the *prayers*" (ESV, italics added for emphasis). Verses 44–46 tell us that this nurturing also included attention to the physical needs of the whole company of disciples. And in verse 46 especially we see that their fellowship together as members of God's new society was a joyful one in their worship and in their relationships with one another.

A well-known bestseller from the early 1980s, *Megatrends* by John Naisbitt, foresaw that in an age of high technology, people would still need to feel cared for and given personal attention. His hypothesis has been borne out by statistics in the twenty-first century that state that nearly half of the population reports feeling alone, left out, or isolated. Ironically, this isolation often stems from social media and virtual relationships, and this has given rise to a renewed desire for real, in-person connection. Most of us have experienced feelings of intense loneliness even when people are close by. We all need the reassurance that we belong—that people care. You could say that in the age of high tech, we're craving "high touch"—close personal connections that move beyond small talk or the surface interactions of liking and commenting on one another's social media posts.

Luke helps us to see in this part of our lesson that these early Christians demonstrated "high touch" in a very practical way. They "lived out" in their day-to-day relationships a deep concern for one another's physical, emotional, and spiritual needs. In this they gave us a greatly needed model for today, as our needs are essentially the same even though more than 2,000 years separate us from their time. Christianity is not a faith that thrives in isolation. We need one another!

A Response to Need and the Results (3:1–4:22)

When that handful of believers in Jerusalem saw the reactions of the crowd during and immediately following Peter's sermon, they undoubtedly felt the pressure of opportunity. In response to their witness, the crowds were asking the right question: "What shall we do?" And in response to an alive and authentic witness for Christ today, that same question is being asked. Behind the masks of smugness and self-sufficiency in our sophisticated society, there is a passionate need to be known and cared for and loved. And when those around us see this kind of Christianity in action, they, too, will ask, "What shall we do?"

Christianity doesn't run into much trouble as long as it minds its own business. It is only when Christians begin to influence their surroundings that reaction and opposition set in. To say that what happened at Pentecost "upset the system" is an understatement, but this next part of our lesson (3:1–4:22) underscores the problems that arose, for here we look at the second pressure faced by those early Christians: the *pressure of censure*.

A Man with a Disability Healed

Luke now moves us quickly into a new drama in which the chief characters are Peter and John and an unnamed man who had such a severe disability that he could not walk. The setting was the Temple, and the time was the ninth hour of the Jewish day—three in the afternoon. It was the time of evening prayer or sacrifice. Peter and John were obviously following their long-established custom of going to the Temple for worship at this hour.

While there, they were confronted at the Temple gate by a disabled man asking them for alms (3:2–3). The scene moves with breathtaking speed to its climax (3:4–6), for Luke tells us that Peter turned his full attention on the needy man and said,

"Silver or gold I do not have, but what I do have I give you. In the name of Jesus Christ of Nazareth, walk" (verse 6, NIV).

Having said that, Peter reached out and touched him. "Taking him by the right hand, he helped him up, and instantly . . . [the man] jumped to his feet and began to walk. Then he went with them into the temple courts, walking and jumping, and praising God" (3:7–8, NIV). Peter and John were used at that moment by the Spirit of God to give the crowd an object lesson on the power that was unleashed on the world by Jesus Christ through His death and resurrection.

Peter and John saw a man with a deep need while they were "on their way" to worship and pray. They didn't view this man as an interruption but as an opportunity, and they acted to meet his need. But in doing so, they created quite a commotion, for the crowd was "filled with wonder and amazement at what had happened to him." The astounded crowd "ran together to them in the portico called Solomon's" (3:10–11, ESV).

Before going on, we should consider an important point. So often we structure our lives with rather fixed agendas. We set goals for what we think we want to do and should do. Then if someone or something unexpectedly diverts our attention, we tend to become impatient or possibly even angry because we've been distracted and interrupted. But again and again Jesus gave us our model for action: no person in need is ever an interruption!

Peter's Second Sermon

It was the upheaval in the crowd over the healing of the disabled man that prompted Peter's second sermon in Luke's sequence of events (3:12–26).

With a boldness that matched the climate of his first sermon on the Day of Pentecost, Peter indicted his listeners for their rejection of Jesus and their role in His crucifixion. But at the same time, Peter signaled Jesus's victory over evil through His resurrection. And once again he gave a ringing call for repentance. Peter then closed his moving appeal by reminding them of God's covenant with Abraham, adding, "God raised up His Servant for you first, and sent Him to bless you by turning every one of you from your wicked ways" (3:26, NASB).

Peter and John Arrested

This sermon of Peter's invoked two kinds of responses (4:1–4). The priests, the captain of the Temple, and the Sadducees descended angrily on the scene, arrested Peter and John because of their word that Jesus had been raised from the dead, and threw them into jail overnight until they could appear before the Sanhedrin.

Now, as then, obedience to the teaching of Jesus and adherence to the Christian faith produces opposition of one kind or another. For some, that opposition may be social, mental, or emotional. For others, even today, it may involve physical restriction or even prison. To not follow the secular status quo isn't popular. But just as the previous part of our lesson gave us an understanding of how to handle positive opportunity, we are now given insight as to how to deal with negative resistance.

On Trial

The scene shifts next to the following morning and to the meeting hall of the Jewish Sanhedrin. After being placed on the witness stand, the disciples were asked, "By what power or by what name did you do this?" (4:7, ESV). In response, Peter launched into an explanation (4:8–12).

First, we see that Peter was courteous. He addressed the Sanhedrin in formal, polite terms. We might describe him as "calm, cool, and collected." But that is the way it is when the Holy Spirit is in control, and Luke tells us that Peter was "filled with the Holy Spirit" (4:8, ESV). Again, we see a sharp contrast to Peter's uncontrolled behavior in the Garden of Gethsemane when he lashed out with a sword against the opposition (John 18:10). This simple difference in action is a profound demonstration of the change that had occurred in Peter's life.

This change in Peter is an illustration of Jesus's words, "Blessed are the meek: for they shall inherit the earth" (Matthew 5:5, KJV). The term for *meek* in the Greek of the New Testament means "one who demonstrates power under control." Peter's calmer response is no indication of passivity, unconcern, or even fatigue after an uncomfortable night in jail. Rather, it is the attitude of one confidently bearing witness to his Lord in the power of the Holy Spirit.

While eagerness to witness for Christ is a good thing, we should caution against allowing our emotions to override our intellect. Agitation and even anger seem to cloud the ability of many otherwise sincere believers today to deal rationally and lovingly with those who do not agree with them. But in this scene Peter is a model of courtesy.

By being "under control," by maintaining a calm and courteous spirit, Peter was better able to give a good defense of his faith. And Peter opened his defense by showing the benefits of the faith and its excellence over other ways of life: "an act of kindness shown to a man who was lame" (4:9, NIV).

This witness to excellence must characterize our interaction with the world around us. It involves excellence of both character and action. This is important because critics of our Christian faith are quick to see through inconsistencies between our expressions of faith and our actions. As Christians, we must keep close watch on our lives and witness to make certain that we are an encouragement and an example to others in their search for faith.

In closing his arguments to the Sanhedrin, Peter made the way of salvation clear for them and us when he said, "Salvation is found in no one else, for there is no other name under heaven given to mankind by which we must be saved" (4:12, NIV). And while we see from the rest of the scene that Peter's witness didn't change their minds, Luke tells us that they marveled at Peter and John's boldness and "they recognized that they had been with Jesus" (4:13, ESV). What a great tribute to the credibility of the two disciples!

But while the Jewish religious leaders were not won over by either Peter's witness or the sight of the healed formerly disabled man, we read that "they could say nothing against it" (4:14, KJV). They couldn't deny the miracle or the strength of Peter's words, but they could try to keep it quiet—to keep Peter and John from speaking and teaching "in the name of Jesus." But Peter's response was clear: their actions would not be regulated by legal decree (4:19–20).

There will undoubtedly be those times when we, as Christians, feel the pressure of opposition. But the qualities demonstrated by Peter and John in this scene can be of help to us as we attempt to handle opposition wherever it may be found. As with the first disciples, the real issue is not *whether* to witness, for, like Peter and John, "we cannot stop speaking about what we have seen and heard" (4:20, NASB). Instead, the real issue is *how* to witness. But we can be certain that when we are sensitive to the Holy Spirit, He will provide not only the opportunity for witness but also the proper attitude and approach.

The Jerusalem Church under Fire (4:23–6:7)

Peter and John's Report

As soon as Peter and John were released from custody, "they went to their own companions and reported everything that the chief priests and the elders had said to them" (4:23, NASB). And following that we have their prayer (4:24–30), their grand affirmation of trust in the Lord, and their determination to speak boldly and to act in the name of Jesus.

A Powerful Unity

Even though the believers then received unusual assurance of the power and providence of God in their behalf (4:31), they did not assume a passive posture when it came to taking care of one another's needs. Spiritual confidence was linked with material concern. They were drawn together in a powerful unity in which Luke says, "Everything was common property and for the use of all" (4:32, AMP). Because of this open spirit among them, no one lacked for anything.

This action by the early Christians has been one of the most controversial parts of the book of Acts. The most common question asked is "Does the Bible teach a sort of Christian communism?" The answer to this must be a quick, clear no! Even a casual student of communism will know that that system was born out of an atheistic presupposition. Actually, the mutual sharing of goods was a direct result of the activity of the Holy Spirit in the hearts of the people. Theirs was not a humanitarianism based simply on noble philosophy or high human motives; it was inspired and directed by the Spirit of God.

A related question is "Does the Bible in this scene teach a Christian commune-ism?" Does it imply that all Christians should sell their possessions and band together in some kind of communal living? Here again, the answer is no. As far as we can tell from the New Testament story of the development of the Early Church, the Jerusalem church was the only one that took this approach. Other congregations met their responsibility to the needy in other ways.

This raises a final question: "Are we then exempted from this particular teaching?" And once again, the answer is no. We are not exempted. But to apply the lesson properly we must distinguish between the *specific* ministry described here and the universal truth it conveys. While no other church in the New Testament seems to have adopted the Jerusalem model, they all demonstrated the same concern for one another. This truth is underlined by Paul in 1 Corinthians 12:25–26: "that there should be no division in the body, but that its parts should have equal concern for each other. If one part suffers, every part suffers with it; if one part is honored, every part rejoices with it" (NIV).

We find in this a principle that is important to us today. In too many churches we not only fail to provide for the needs of others in the congregation, but we also don't even know their names. The Early Church was a community of believers who knew and cared for one another. And even though the church in Jerusalem now had several thousand members, they found a way to know those who were in need and minister to them.

At the same time, the book of Acts is very realistic. In 6:1–8, we see that this system, though admirable, was not perfect. Even though this takes us out of the natural sequence, take a moment now and read those verses in your Bible. Luke shows us here how the Christian community responded when its program was inadequate. The Greek-speaking Jewish converts complained that they were being overlooked in the daily distribution. They appealed for attention and support, and the church responded. In doing so, we see two important principles for us today.

First, the believers stopped any form of preferential treatment. Cultural, linguistic, and racial differences were not allowed to determine the distribution of aid. And second, they took action to put priorities in perspective. If everyone was involved in the daily distribution, the tasks of prayer and the ministry of the Word would collapse. Some division of labor was needed so the apostles could be free to devote themselves to prayer and the Word. To meet the needs of the community, a new order of men with good reputations, who were wise and full of the Holy Spirit, was formed. They were called deacons, and Stephen was part of this group. (While the Acts account restricts this designation to men, a woman named Phoebe was in fact called a deacon in Paul's letter to the Roman church [Romans 16:1–2].)

Deception at Work

The book of Acts never glosses over the imperfection of Christians. This adds to the sense of realism we get when we read it. No sooner had the early Christians dealt with the pressure of providing for those in need than they had to turn their attention to handling the pressure of deception (5:1–11).

Here is a vivid story of deceit and dishonesty. Despite some popular misunderstanding, the problem of Ananias and Sapphira was not that they withheld part of their money for themselves. There is no indication that believers were required or forced to put everything in a pool for the common support. Rather, the problem was that this couple lied to the church by implying that what they gave was all they had—that they had given everything they owned. It was the lie, not the amount or the choice to give a certain amount, that brought the condemnation. Peter's words were very strong: "Ananias, how is it that Satan has so filled your heart that you have lied to the Holy Spirit and have kept for yourself some of the money you received for the land? Didn't it belong to you before it was sold? And after it was sold, wasn't the money at your disposal? What made you think of doing such a thing? You have not lied just to human beings but to God" (5:3–4, NIV).

The story of Ananias and Sapphira is a cautionary account for believers today. Ananias and Sapphira fell into the trap of wanting to be seen as giving all. More than likely this couple had seen the accolades and respect heaped upon those who gave all of their possessions and resources to the church and wanted that admiration themselves.

This story can teach us several important lessons: First, we must be honest with ourselves, with others, and with God about the gifts we give to ministry. Second, we must avoid the pitfalls of seeking glory for the work we do for the church and for the Lord—or put another way, doing work for the church and the Lord with the motivation and hopes of receiving praise or recognition. Third, our giving should be done without the expectation of honor or accolades—and it is best kept between you, your church leadership, and God. And finally, the church itself should avoid drawing attention to or gushing over those of means who give large, "splashy" gifts to the church, to avoid resentment or feelings of inadequacy from others in the congregation whose resources are more limited.

The proper spirit for giving is described by Jesus in the story of the widow's mite (Luke 21:1–4). While she gave all she had, it wasn't much. It was the spirit in which she gave that mattered to Jesus, not the amount. Luke may well have had that story in mind as he wrote about the deception of Ananias and Sapphira. These two stories illustrate the sacredness of our stewardship. Our giving to the Lord and His cause is not done to impress people or for income-tax deduction—it is a sacred matter between ourselves and God. To be dishonest, to give with a wrong spirit, is to fall prey to the pressure of deception.

Faith under Fire

As we read and study this part of our lesson, we begin to sense the progression of intensity that Luke is describing.

Beginning with the positive pressure of opportunity, we have now moved to the actual pressure of confinement. Even as the church was growing rapidly (5:12–16) and many miracles were being performed, the Jewish leaders stepped in with their most forceful resistance to date. They "arrested the apostles and put them in the public prison" (5:18, ESV).

Why were they jailed? Surely it was not because people were healed or the kingdom of God was advanced. The issue here is much more subtle. The high priest and his compatriots "were filled with jealousy and resentment" (5:17, AMP) because the apostles continued to teach in Jesus's name and were, in effect, bypassing the established system. Their movement was "unofficial" and thus should be squelched even if some good was coming out of it.

This section in Acts 5:12–42 reveals some very important lessons for us. First, we need to face the truth that God isn't limited in the ways He acts. He may do it "our way," or He may do it in a completely new and different way. God is not limited by our understanding of Him. But the Jewish leaders based all their assumptions on the idea that God was bound to act through the approved religious system or at least in ways predictably consistent with the Jewish tradition. The assumption was wrong. By holding tenaciously to that assumption, the religious leaders not only remained blind but also actually worked against the purposes of God!

The second lesson for us here is expressed in the words of the apostles themselves: "We must obey God rather than human beings!" (5:29, NIV). This was not a super-pious statement made to impress anybody. Instead, it was an honest statement of their conviction and was the result of a long period of walking with Jesus Himself and being instructed by Him after the resurrection. By the time they said these words, they knew to whom they belonged and to what they were called. They were firm in their belief, but it was a firmness based on fact, not stubbornness.

Stubbornness isn't a mark of spirituality, but deep commitment is. And that is what the disciples exhibited on this occasion. It is important to notice, too, that they were talking in this instance to unbelievers and not to their brothers and sisters in Christ.

At any rate, we see that God honored their courage, and they were delivered from prison (5:19). This kind of confirmation left no doubt about what position they should take before their accusers. We can believe that when our response is correct and in the right spirit, it will be confirmed in some way by God. If we are truly obeying God rather than humans, we shall obey Him when He tells us to stick to our guns, and we shall obey Him when He shows us we are wrong and need to confess it.

Again, Peter and the other apostles gave their accusers a forthright witness to the Saviorhood of Jesus and the power of the Holy Spirit. But Luke tells us the religious leaders were "furious" (5:33, NIV) and discussed their intention of killing the apostles. Now the story takes an interesting turn. Gamaliel, a widely loved member of the Sanhedrin, and a Pharisee, attempted wisely to intervene and prevent violence. Likening this to certain other recent events, he offered good advice: "If their purpose or activity is of human origin, it will fail. But if it is from God, you will not be able to stop these men" (5:38–39, NIV). In this instance, the group agreed with Gamaliel and released the apostles with a flogging—which would have been horrifically painful and incapacitating for a time, almost certainly leaving terrible scars—and an admonition to keep quiet.

Running through the narrative is an interesting possibility. Gamaliel was the very person who had instructed Saul of Tarsus. And we know from the last part of this lesson that Saul was present at the stoning of Stephen. It is even possible he witnessed this scene we've been discussing. The point is simply this: long before the apostles ever knew that their faith was having any impact on the opposition, it was!

Faithful unto Death (6:1–8:3)

The final pressure faced by the early Christians was that of martyrdom, as demonstrated by Stephen in Acts 6:8–8:3. The fact that Luke devotes so much space to this event reveals its importance then and now. People today are still being martyred for their faith. So as we read these words in Acts, we hear a message that is significant for us even today.

The First Christian Martyr

The first thing of importance to us here is to see the sinister and active nature of evil (6:8–12). At the synagogue, when Stephen's opponents in debate saw that they were beaten, they dredged up some witnesses who perjured themselves by claiming that Stephen made certain heretical statements.

Based on this flimsy evidence, Stephen was arrested and taken before the Sanhedrin. But as we shall see, the power of evil, though immediately victorious, could not thwart the spread of the gospel.

The second thing of importance to us is to notice that Stephen was prepared. He was ready in attitude and countenance (6:15), and he was ready in message and content (7:1–53). The sermon he preached followed a course similar to those we've already seen in this lesson. And it had a similar outcome, only this time the consequences were more severe. The contrast between Stephen and his listeners is glaring (7:54–60). His listeners were full of hatred; Stephen was full of the Holy Spirit. His listeners were intent on murder; Stephen was intent on forgiving. They called on their anger; he called on his God. They departed in rage; he died in peace—the first Christian martyr.

And Saul of Tarsus saw it all! In fact, some commentators suspect that Saul played a more direct role in the dastardly event (7:58). That Luke saw fit to add that "Saul approved of [Stephen's] execution" (8:1, ESV) makes this all the more probable. As we view this whole event from our perspective today, it is clear that God used Saul's presence and possible participation in the affair to impact his life and prepare him for his forthcoming conversion. St. Augustine was correct when he wrote, "The church owes Paul to the prayer of Stephen."

The events in this lesson demonstrate that it is too easy to think that growth takes place in times of security and ease. More than that, it is easy to interpret comfort and prosperity as signs of God's blessing. Clearly, God's blessing was on the church during this time, but it was still a difficult time. Yet the final message is one of hope: *You can grow under pressure.* In fact, it seems that most of the time, our growth and maturity come when we are under pressure.

Dear Lord, when I am under pressure, help me grow in grace and faith as the early believers did. AMEN.

INSPIRATION FROM THE BOOK OF ACTS

While they were stoning him, Stephen prayed, "Lord Jesus, receive my spirit." Then he fell on his knees and cried out, "Lord, do not hold this sin against them." When he had said this, he fell asleep.

—Acts 7:59–60, NIV

"Can a person change?" I asked Jesus in prayer one night. "More to the point, can I change? Will I ever become more like You?"

I was frustrated with myself. I'd begun the day with great intentions to be a faithful servant of Christ but slipped into old patterns of worry, selfishness, and discouragement. Some days it feels like the older I get, the less I'm being conformed to the likeness of Christ, when I long for the opposite.

I wonder if Stephen ever asked similar questions. If so, I found a surprising answer in Acts 7. As Stephen was dying—unjustly attacked, in horrible pain—he prayed for those stoning him. My human nature would be tempted to pray, "Smite them!" But Stephen used similar words to the ones Jesus used on the Cross in Luke 23:34: "Father, forgive them, for they do not know what they are doing" (NIV). In his moments of greatest distress, Stephen emulated Jesus and trusted Jesus to receive his spirit.

His story gives me great hope. Jesus can indeed live through us. Not through our own feeble efforts but through His grace. Like Stephen, we may find words coming from us that are straight from the heart of Christ. We may respond in a way that supersedes our human nature. We can give our spirit to Jesus one day when we face death, and we can also give ourselves to Him each day of our lives.

—Sharon Hinck

Notes

Notes

LESSON 3: ACTS 8:4–12:25

Expanding the Territory

God, help me to tell more and more people about Your love. AMEN.

God never intended for the Christian movement to be confined to Jerusalem. More than likely, the disciples knew that. On at least two occasions, Jesus had challenged them with a vision for the world (Matthew 28:19 and Acts 1:8) that reached the ends of the earth. It is also possible that during those forty days of teaching and preparation between His resurrection and ascension, Jesus shared with His disciples the vision of the expansion of the Christian faith. Whether or not He gave them a specific plan for that expansion can only be a matter of speculation since the Scripture passage doesn't give us a clue.

What we do know as we study this lesson is that this section of the book of Acts takes place on a new stage. Using Acts 1:8 as a key verse for understanding the book, we know that Jesus predicted the spread of Christianity from Jerusalem, to Judea and Samaria, and ultimately to the ends of the earth: "You will be my witnesses in Jerusalem, and in all Judea and Samaria, and to the ends of the earth" (NIV).

The events in the first seven chapters of Acts confine Christian activity largely to Jerusalem. In our lesson now, though, we see the Good News spreading throughout Judea and into Samaria. Here we see the church on the move. Never again would geographical, racial, or cultural boundaries impede the movement of God's new fellowship.

As we study this lesson, it is possible to find an organizing verse in Acts 8:4: "Now those who were scattered went about preaching the word" (ESV). Luke is showing us here, through the ministry of several key people, how the church expanded its territory under the leadership of the Spirit. And from this we shall discover certain strategies that can help us as we seek to expand the Christian faith in our day.

But first we need to look at the circumstances that precipitated this outward-moving process. Luke tells us that the stoning of Stephen was the beginning of "a great persecution against the church" (8:1, KJV), and then he adds, "Saul began ravaging the church, entering house after house; and he would drag away men and women and put them in prison" (8:3, NASB). Here is a picture of brutality. The harassment of the Christians was ferocious—they were dragged from their homes and thrown into prison (8:3).

It was this violent persecution that forced the Christians to leave Jerusalem and seek refuge in the surrounding countryside of Judea and Samaria. But remember, the Jerusalem church membership already ran into the thousands. This was no small exodus—it was a mass migration, an event of significance. And its significance is increased when we read that even though they were a persecuted people, they did not shrink from preaching and teaching about Jesus wherever they went.

What an amazing sequence of events! In an effort to squelch the Christian witness, Stephen is killed and Saul of Tarsus tries to throw all the Christians into prison or frighten them into silence. But instead, the apostles continue their witness boldly in Jerusalem while thousands of other Christians move out to infiltrate the surrounding countryside.

Luke's selection of characters in this drama is important to the story. Three men—Philip, Peter, and Paul—stand out above everyone else. Not only were they three outstanding leaders, but they were also three examples of the Spirit's ability to use people. Peter, of course, was representative of the apostles—the established ministry of the time. These were, in effect, the "ordained clergy." Philip was one of the "new ministers," one of the seven deacons referred to in chapter six. And there was Paul (aka Saul), probably selected as a prime example of how God can use the most unlikely people in His service. These lead characters in the Christian drama symbolize the traditional, the innovative, and the surprising ways God works to accomplish His will.

The Glorious Gospel (8:4–8:40)

There's an old phrase that asks, "Yes, but will it play in Peoria?" It is meant to describe something that works in one place but might not in another. That's the question Acts 8:5–40 answers.

The Gospel in Samaria

No sooner had the Christian believers been dispersed than Philip went "down to a city in Samaria and proclaimed the

Messiah there" (8:5, NIV). It is quite likely this refers to Samaria's principal city of that time—the ancient city of Samaria that had been rebuilt by Herod and renamed Sebaste. But the important thing to note here is that Philip boldly went with his message of salvation into an area where the people were violently antagonistic to anything related to Judaism, and that would have included Christianity at that time. The bitter hostility between Jews and Samaritans was several hundred years old, and we see evidence of that tension in the Gospel account of the woman at the well (John 4) and the parable of the good Samaritan (Luke 10:25–37).

It is for this reason that Philip's move into Samaria had particular significance. It was a landmark event because it proved that the gospel was not just for a select number of Jerusalem Jews but was for everyone—even Samaritans.

It is equally remarkable to see the widespread reception to Philip's message and actions on the part of the Samaritans (8:6–8). But this is just another indication of the radical newness of Christianity. New Christians (converted Jews) were going places they had previously avoided and were sharing their Good News with people they had previously despised. And they were received with open arms! In fact, Luke says, "And there was great joy in that city" (8:8, KJV). The Samaritans passed a true test of Christianity: They were full of joy. Then and now authentic Christianity produces people who are full of joy, not doom and gloom.

In the midst of this joyful setting, a minor character entered the scene. His name was Simon, and he was a magician, a sorcerer. Luke indicates that as a result of Philip's preaching, Simon became a believer and was baptized (8:13). Philip apparently felt that Simon's conversion was genuine, and since Simon already had a following (8:9), he could have a positive influence. At this point in the story, Luke tells us that Simon "continued with Philip. And seeing signs and great miracles performed, he was amazed" (8:13, ESV).

But it wasn't long before things changed. When the apostles back in Jerusalem got word about what was happening in Samaria, they sent Peter and John to confirm and affirm the results of Philip's ministry (8:14). After seeing what had happened, Peter and John prayed that the new Samaritan converts would receive the Holy Spirit, and, as Luke writes, the apostles "laid their hands on them and they received the Holy Spirit" (8:17, ESV).

The laying on of hands by Peter and John and the reception of the Holy Spirit by the new converts made a strong impression on Simon. This exceeded anything he'd ever been able to do as a magician, and his baser instincts rose to the surface. Offering Peter and John money, he asked, "Give me also this ability so that everyone on whom I lay my hands may receive the Holy Spirit" (8:19, NIV).

Peter's response to Simon (8:20–23) is a strong denunciation. The gift of the Holy Spirit was not for sale.

We might title this part of our Scripture lesson "Glorious, but Not for Sale." Simon's real tragedy was not that he had asked (though that's bad enough); instead, it was that he had thought the power of God could be purchased with human means. He had failed to see that what was happening was not the property of any person—it was the activity of a sovereign

God. Two thousand years later we still need to remember that. There's not enough money in the world to get a corner on God's blessing and the work of the Holy Spirit. The Spirit still moves where and when He wills.

We leave this tragic scene with Simon crying for mercy (8:24–25). While Simon's words here may indicate repentance, we do not know for sure. But we do know that from his name comes our modern term *simony*—the making of profit from sacred things—a despicable act now even as it was then.

Our Scripture lesson further tells us that the gospel continued to produce converts in other Samaritan cities (8:25). And so, the answer to the question asked at the beginning of this section is, "Yes, it *will* play in Peoria!" The gospel of Jesus Christ is effective wherever it goes despite problems and even perversions. For more than 2,000 years, the picture of the Christian church has often been blurred and discolored by the words and actions of people who dishonor the spirit of Jesus. And at times certain groups within the church have resorted to physical and verbal violence in the so-called defense of the faith. But in the face of human sin, God is still in charge; His will and purposes prevail.

Taking the Gospel to Gaza and Ethiopia

Luke now moves us abruptly from Samaria south to a busy highway. We read: "Now an angel of the Lord said to Philip, 'Rise and go toward the south to the road that goes down from Jerusalem to Gaza.' This is a desert place" (8:26, ESV). The road Luke is referring to stretched south and west from Jerusalem by way of Bethlehem and Hebron and continued on southwest toward the coast, where it connected below Gaza with the highly traveled highway to Egypt.

It was to this highway that Philip was instructed to go. Philip apparently had no idea why he was going; he was merely told to go. And he did. What a marvelous lesson in obedience! Many, if not most, of us would have argued with the angel. We would have wanted a plan of action. But God doesn't always work that way. In Philip we have a model for obeying the word of the Lord without question.

The scene shifts now to the desert highway. And it was there Philip came upon an Ethiopian man who was sitting in his chariot and reading from an Isaiah scroll. With his careful attention to detail, Luke tells us that the Ethiopian was a eunuch and attached to the court of Candace—or "the Kandake (which means 'queen of the Ethiopians')," as the New International Version translates it (8:27)—as the royal treasurer. The Ethiopia mentioned here is not located where we know it today but was situated on the Nile River in what is now Sudan.

Philip was next instructed by the Spirit of the Lord to join the man in the chariot. He did, and then follows the story in which Philip explained the Scripture to his fellow traveler. This led to the Ethiopian's conversion and baptism (8:28–39). And from there, through this new convert, the gospel spread toward the heart of Africa.

There are many obvious lessons to be drawn from this story. But let's focus especially on the point of our responsiveness to the Holy Spirit. We see that Philip was led by the Spirit in this rendezvous with the Ethiopian. And most certainly one key to our discipleship is our willingness to listen to and heed the "nudges" of the Spirit. As we obey those nudges—that guidance—we, too, may be led to be of help, a witness, to people in need. Along with Philip we will have the opportunity to point a searcher toward Jesus Christ.

Through Philip, Luke has shown us a glorious gospel of Good News—one that works when it is applied. This is not to say that we will always ride the crest of success. There will be down moments of resistance and difficulty. But this part of our lesson provides ample hope for us to believe that Christianity can reach people where they are and bring them into a saving relationship with God.

A Sudden and Surprising Surrender (9:1–9:31)

Twice before, Luke, in line with his unique literary style, has planted mention of a man who now becomes the central figure in one of the greatest dramas in Christian history (9:1–8). We first met Saul when he witnessed Stephen's death. He is then described as creating havoc within the Christian community. Now Luke moves Saul onto center stage, and he is "still breathing threats and murder against the disciples of the Lord" (9:1, NASB).

A Mission of Vengeance

But Saul of Tarsus was no ordinary religious fanatic. Born in Tarsus in Cilicia, young Saul had been raised in an intellectual atmosphere flavored with Greek thought and rich in the culture of this ancient city. From such a rich background he would have been able to draw from the noblest teaching in the Graeco-Roman world.

From that heritage Saul moved on to Jerusalem, where he became a student of Rabbi Gamaliel, one of the greatest Jewish teachers of that time. It isn't surprising that Saul advanced rapidly, and as a zealous Pharisee, he had become a sworn enemy of the Christians.

It is apparent that some Jewish Christians had migrated to the city of Damascus, at that time an independent metropolis situated within the boundaries of the Nabatean kingdom. Obviously, Saul had heard about this Christian community, and armed with papers of extradition, he set out to apprehend them and bring them back to Jerusalem for punishment.

It is quite likely that Saul's route on this mission of vengeance took him north from Jerusalem through Samaria to just south of the Sea of Galilee where he crossed the Jordan River. It is likely that he headed north through the vicinity of Gadara and over the Golan Heights, where he would then have moved north and east toward Damascus. In all, the distance was probably between 135 and 150 miles and would have involved six to eight days of rather rigorous travel. The strenuousness of the journey indicates Saul's vehemence.

A Dramatic Confrontation

Saul of Tarsus is without doubt the last person mentioned so far that we would expect to become a Christian. Yet Luke tells us that as Saul and his party were getting close to Damascus, he had a dramatic confrontation with One who identified Himself as "Jesus, whom you are persecuting" (9:5, ESV).

Saul's excessive and compulsive zeal and anger may well have been the outward sign of inner torture. There's much about the Saul of those days that we don't know, but we do know that on that Damascus road, the grace of God shone brightly, and Saul was converted.

If you have been referring to the King James Version alongside other translations in our study, you will notice two discrepancies (beyond the differences in wording)—two elements in the King James Version that are missing from modern translations. Jesus's statement to Saul, "It is hard for thee to kick against the pricks" (9:5, KJV), and Saul's question, "Lord, what wilt thou have me to do?" (9:6, KJV) are excluded from modern versions. Bible commentators note that these statements were likely added by later copyists or scribes to align with the later accounts in which Paul is telling his own story—found in Acts 22:10 and 26:14. The earliest manuscripts do not include them in chapter 9, so the modern translations leave them out.

This account of Jesus confronting Paul on the road, of course, is a familiar story to Christians everywhere, so much so that a "Damascus road experience" has come to mean any dramatic turnaround or life-altering transformation. Unfortunately, some have used Paul's experience across the years as the "model" for all conversions. There is much cause for us to rejoice in Saul's experience, but it is wrong to consider it normal for everyone else. What is normal, though, is the ability of God to break through even the most hostile and stubborn defenses and to win us to Himself. This event is a marvelous reminder that no one is beyond the reach of God!

In this next part of our story (9:10–19) we come to the confirmation of what happened. Let's look at how this was worked out.

The Lord next told Saul to go into Damascus (9:6) and wait for further instructions. This he did, but since he had been blinded by his encounter with God, he had to be led in by those who were with him. And Luke next tells us that he waited three days—blind, refusing to eat or drink—before he received any further word.

The Lord's Special Messenger

Once again the scene shifts, and it goes to a man named Ananias, a resident of Damascus, whom the Lord had selected to be the one to confirm the conversion of Saul (9:10–18). It is hard for us to realize how much Ananias risked in obeying the Lord and going to Saul. He put his life on the line in approaching the very person who was arresting and imprisoning Christians.

I'm quite sure he was willing to obey the Lord and go to Straight Street because he was a man of prayer. Ananias had to know a deep level of communion with God to be willing to take the risk involved. It is interesting to compare the dialogue here between God and Ananias (9:11–16) with the conversation between God and Moses in Exodus 3. Take just a minute and turn back to the third chapter of Exodus and make the comparison. The outcome is much the same, isn't it? In both of these stories we receive our own confirmation of the truth that when God gives us an assignment, we can be sure that He will give us whatever it takes to complete that assignment.

Imagine, if you can, this next scene. Saul has been waiting—alone. His world has been turned upside down. What would happen next? The door opens, and he hears someone walking up to him. Silence. And then, "*Brother Saul,* the Lord—Jesus, who appeared to you on the road as you were coming here—has sent me so that you may see again and be filled with the Holy Spirit" (9:17, NIV, italics added for emphasis). Once Saul had been an enemy; now he is a brother.

Saul Preaches in the Synagogues

Luke seems to hurry on as if he can't wait to tell us the rest of the story. Saul receives his sight back, he is physically restored, and he enjoys a newfound fellowship with the other believers in Damascus—his new status as a brother in Christ having been affirmed by them.

Then we come to the final confirmation of what happened through Saul's own testimony: "Immediately he proclaimed Jesus in the synagogues, saying, 'He is the Son of God'" (9:20, ESV). That certainly signals the completeness of Saul's conversion: He preached Christ to the very people who had once been his allies in hating Christians. Their response was understandable (9:21). But Saul held steady with his message, "and confounded the Jews who lived in Damascus by proving that Jesus was the Christ" (9:22, ESV).

We move now to the next part of the story—the challenge. It was only a matter of time until Saul's old cronies had taken all they could. An ominous note is sounded as Luke writes, "There was a conspiracy among the Jews to kill him" (9:23, NIV). Silencing the opposition has always been a tactic of evil. One article estimated that every day, thirteen Christians are killed because of their faith, and another twelve are unjustly imprisoned because of it. Some estimates suggest that more than 300,000 Christians around the world face serious persecution for their faith. Still others have been ostracized by their families and friends because they have become Christians. The challenge then and now is inevitable—in Saul's case it was extreme.

But God was just beginning his work with Saul, and so the plans of his enemies were thwarted and he escaped (9:24–25). His problems weren't over just yet, however; he still had to face the challenge of acceptance by the Christians in Jerusalem (9:26–31).

Here were people who had felt the sting of Saul's persecution. It is likely that many had seen him standing in approval at the death of Stephen. They could remember firsthand his threats and violent acts. It is not surprising they were afraid and unwilling to accept him.

Once again it was necessary for someone to vouch for Saul's legitimacy. This time it was Barnabas who pleaded Saul's case (9:27). And this was the beginning of a long relationship between Saul and Barnabas that God would use to spread the gospel. Obviously, the word of Barnabas was trusted because Saul was now welcomed into the fellowship at Jerusalem.

This part of our lesson ends with an important summary verse (9:31) that tells of the expansion of the church throughout Judea, Galilee, and Samaria. And it also indicates that the Christian believers "enjoyed a time of peace and [were] strengthened . . . and encouraged by the Holy Spirit" (NIV).

After the fast-paced events of this part of our lesson, it is heartening to know that there may come periods of calm.

The Gospel for Everyone (9:32–11:30)

As in a movie, when the director cuts to another scene, Luke now suddenly shifts characters and settings. Peter returns to center stage, and we read that he was traveling from place to place preaching the gospel of salvation through faith in Jesus Christ to the Jews (9:32). We have already seen through the ministry of Philip and Saul (Paul) that the Good News was being well received. Up to now, however, the strategy of the Christians had been to win converts from Judaism. But in this part of our lesson a new thrust emerges: Gentiles, as well, are seen to be potential recipients of the gospel. The glorious gospel not only reaches such unlikely people as Saul, but it also penetrates unlikely cultures and races. In fact, we see from this part of the story that the word *unlikely* is erased from the Christian dictionary. For us, of course, over 2,000 years later, there is nothing unlikely or unusual about the idea that the gospel of Jesus recognizes no social, racial, or geographic boundaries. But in those early morning hours of the Christian movement, it was still thought to be only for Jews, wherever they lived.

Peter in Lydda and Joppa

We pick up Peter now as he joins "the Lord's people who lived in Lydda" (9:32, NIV)—a town west and slightly north of Jerusalem on the road to the seacoast and the port of Joppa (now called Jaffa). Here we see Peter acting in Jesus's name as he is instrumental in the healing of a paralyzed man by the name of Aeneas (9:33).

As we might expect, word of this healing got around—even to Joppa on the coast. So we read next that when a Christian in Joppa named Tabitha (Dorcas in Greek) died, her fellow Christians asked Peter to "Please come at once!" (9:38, NIV). In response to their request, Peter left Lydda and traveled the 10 miles to Joppa, where, after he prayed, Tabitha's life was restored (9:40–41).

Peter's ministry in these two cities was, in a sense, preparatory for the next major event in his life and ministry. But there are two things in the Lydda and Joppa stories we should examine before we go any further. First, the words used to describe both the believers in Lydda (verse 32) and those in Joppa (verse 41)—"saints (God's people)" in the Amplified Version and "the Lord's people" and "the believers" in the New International Version—come from a Greek word that means "different." In other words, the Christians, the saints, were different in belief and behavior from the non-Christians.

Second, we see in these two stories that God continues to be able and willing to meet the needs of people and of His church. The miracles performed in these two stories were vehicles by which others came to believe in Christ. But it is important to notice that Peter was not on some sort of a miracle bandwagon. He wasn't engaged in a traveling miracle show. The miracles simply occurred in the natural course of his ministry, and those who saw what happened were convinced of the authenticity of Christianity.

For Peter personally, these events were necessary as a further reminder of the sovereign ability of God to do whatever He chooses. The restoration of life to Tabitha revealed a God who can overrule even death itself. And Peter's ongoing realization that "God can do whatever He wants to do" was essential in preparing him for the series of events that were soon to come in this next part of our lesson.

Introducing Cornelius the Centurion

Once again Luke cuts to another scene. Some 35 miles north of Joppa was the thriving port city of Caesarea, the seat of the Roman government in Palestine. Now a new character moves into the Christian drama: "At Caesarea there was a man named Cornelius, a centurion of what was known as the Italian Cohort" (10:1, ESV).

Cornelius, we are told, was a devout man—a man who abandoned a belief in polytheism (many gods) and was searching for the true God. Luke tells us that he "prayed to God continually" (10:2, NASB)—he was already a man of prayer. And it was while he was praying one day that an angel appeared to him, affirmed his prayers and good works, and instructed him to make contact with Peter, who at that moment was just a few miles south in Joppa. Cornelius then dispatched two servants and an aide to find Peter (10:2–9).

Peter's Vision

Act two in this drama opens with Peter at noon prayer. First, God had been in communication with Cornelius; now He is working on Peter through a vision (10:9–17). With his keen descriptive sense, Luke takes us into the scene. Peter saw what appeared to be a sheet coming down from heaven, and in it "all kinds of animals and reptiles and birds of the air" (10:12, ESV). Then a voice told him to kill and eat. Peter was horrified—he still adhered to the dietary restrictions of Judaism. Although the voice from heaven assured him that in God's sight nothing was unclean, Peter did not respond. The scene was repeated twice more before it disappeared, but Peter still failed to understand (10:17).

God's timing, though, is always so right. For while Peter was pondering what had happened, the three messengers from Cornelius arrived and told him all about the angel's visit to Cornelius. Peter then fed them and put them up for the night while he got ready to go with them to Caesarea.

God initiated this new and essential phase of the universal mission of the gospel with two men—Cornelius and Peter—who were devoted to prayer. Earlier, Luke gave us the example of Ananias, another prayerful man who was trusted with an important mission. We learn from this that the deep and significant things of God are for those who spend time in prayer.

During the height of the mid-twentieth-century "space race," in which the United States and the Soviet Union grappled with each other to gain supremacy in space, one of the Soviet cosmonauts made an arrogant and senseless statement, saying that he hadn't seen God anywhere during the time he was in space. In response, a Russian Orthodox priest wisely said that we shouldn't be surprised that the astronaut failed to see God in space. "You cannot expect someone to see God in space who has not first seen Him on earth," he pointed out.

Neither could we expect the disciples to be in a position to see, hear, and try such radical new ideas unless they had first established deep and meaningful connections with the Spirit of God. And in the context of the rest of the story, we know that through Peter's prayer and his vision, he was uniquely prepared for this drastic new step. His doubts were erased with the appearance of the messengers from Cornelius and the words of the Holy Spirit: "Go with them, doubting nothing: for I have sent them" (10:20, KJV).

The Conversion of Cornelius and His Household

God had spoken. In fact, He had to speak to Peter more than once through the vision. But that didn't matter. The important thing was that now Peter obeyed. And what matters most for us is that we obey God, for His will and purposes are accomplished by people who obey Him.

Next we travel with Peter to Caesarea and to the home of Cornelius. And here comes the proof that Peter finally understood what God had been trying to tell him: "You yourselves know how unlawful it is for a Jew to associate with or to visit anyone of another nation, but God has shown me that I should not call any person common or unclean" (10:28, ESV).

With that introduction Luke gives us a full account of what happened (10:24–48). The seeker is reached by the obedient disciple, and this is followed by a clear presentation of the message of salvation through Christ and the attentiveness of Cornelius and his household. And right in the middle of this scene, the Holy Spirit came—just as He had come to the believers on the Day of Pentecost. For the hearers, it was the fulfillment of their desire to know God more fully. For Peter, it was proof positive that "God is not one to show partiality, but in every nation the one who fears Him and does what is right is acceptable to Him" (10:34–35, NASB).

This message is relevant today. Inside the Christian church there is still a spirit of exclusiveness that rears its ugly head and insists that "different people" or people with different ideas are not prime candidates for "our group." To be sure, we would deny this most of the time, but we confirm it by our actions and attitudes. We need to be reminded daily that God *still* "does not show favoritism" (verse 35, NIV).

Peter's Defense

In this next part of the lesson, we see just how difficult it was for those early Jewish Christians to understand what was happening (11:1–18). When word of what had happened at Caesarea got back to the Jewish Christians in Jerusalem, they really got nervous. So when Peter returned, they held him to account. Peter had broken the sacred traditions by eating with an uncircumcised Gentile. And at this point we must remember that the early Christians, all of whom were Jews or Jewish converts, still tended to understand their new faith in Jesus in terms of their ancestral faith.

The "circumcision group" just couldn't believe that Peter would dare go to those who were uncircumcised. By their standards, even though Cornelius feared God, he was not a candidate for salvation. But to emphasize the importance of this whole issue, Luke goes into considerable detail here. Peter recounted the entire sequence of events at Joppa and at Caesarea, and then in telling how the Holy Spirit came to the household of Cornelius, he recalled for them the words of Jesus: "John baptized with water, but you will be baptized with the Holy Spirit" (11:16, ESV).

We have in Peter's defense here a straightforward plea for understanding—a presentation of truth. And it was accepted as such, for Luke now writes, "When they heard this, they had no further objections and praised God, saying, 'So then, even to Gentiles God has granted repentance that leads to life'" (11:18, NIV).

The Church at Antioch

The rest of Acts 11 gives us two other lessons on the theme that the gospel of Jesus is for everyone. First, we see further confirmation of the fact that Gentiles were to be included in God's new fellowship of believers (11:19–26).

As the scene shifts to the metropolis of Antioch, we find that not only was the gospel preached there but it was well received. This was most significant since Antioch ranked with Alexandria and Rome in importance in the then-known world. It was a major center of culture and of pagan worship of the goddess Daphne. Antioch was also known as a center of immorality, but it was here that the gospel took firm root and where believers were first called Christians (11:26).

One in Spirit

The second lesson that comes to us now has to do with the intense connection that existed among the believers (11:27–30). They cared for and about one another. This is illustrated by the visit of Agabus to Antioch. When he told the Christians there about the threatened famine in Judea, they immediately banded together and provided generous relief. They were one in the Spirit and one in the Lord. The wall between Jew and Gentile was broken down. Christianity was on the verge of becoming a world religion.

The important lesson for us here is to know that while the gospel is inclusive, it does not gloss over immorality or indecent behavior. But it does include *everyone* who repents of sin, accepts Jesus Christ as Savior and Lord, and lives consistently with that commitment. For all of these "old things are passed away; behold, all things are become new" (2 Corinthians 5:17, KJV).

Growing Pains (12:1–12:25)

The Death of James and Peter's Arrest

The adage "The blood of martyrs is the seed of the church" is certainly confirmed in Acts 12. To please the Jewish religious leaders, Herod Agrippa launched an attack on the Christian community in Jerusalem. "He had James the brother of John executed with a sword" (12:2, NASB), and he threw Peter into prison (12:3). The period of calm referred to in 9:31 was over, and a campaign of intense persecution was leveled against the Christians.

But amid this time of testing we catch something of the mood of the church: "So Peter was kept in prison, but *earnest prayer for him was made to God* by the church" (12:5, ESV, italics added for emphasis). In times of difficulty, stress, and persecution, victory comes through prayer. This is not pious sentimentalism; it is raw truth. Up to this point in our lesson we've seen prayer as the vehicle for service and ministry. Now we see it as the means to deliver and defend Christianity against its enemies.

But prayer should never be interpreted as sort of a magic cure-all. It is not a divine vending machine into which we drop requests and get back answers. Rather, prayer is communion with God that strengthens us in our faith whether the results in the moment are what we expected or not. In the face of evil, prayer will help us rise above our difficulties and suffering to see the God who is still with us.

Peter Delivered

In Peter's case, the church prayed and a miracle occurred (12:6–11): An angel of the Lord freed Peter and led him out to the street. When he appeared at the locked door where the Christians were praying for him, it created quite a commotion. The girl Rhoda answered the door and recognized Peter, but she was so surprised that she forgot to let him in, and she ran back to tell the others that Peter was outside. But they refused to believe her (12:15). Even though they had been praying for Peter, they evidently hadn't expected this kind of an answer. So Peter had to keep knocking until they finally opened up for him. There's a twist of humor in this scene, but how often are we like those Christians that night? We pray and then we're "astonished" (12:16, NIV) when the Lord answers.

God was making an important point here for those early Christians: prison bars, evil plots, and even murder cannot stop the movement of the faith. Luke underlines this truth in these significant words: "The word of God grew and multiplied" (12:24, KJV).

Christianity had now moved out beyond Judea and Samaria. This is a vivid story of the expansion of faith in Jesus Christ. True, it didn't happen without problems, perversions, and persecution. But there was no attitude of defeat among these early believers. In fact, our Scripture lesson closes with the word that Saul (Paul) and Barnabas and young John Mark were getting ready to leave on what we commonly refer to as Paul's first missionary journey.

In our lesson we have seen that unlikely people, unlikely races, and unlikely circumstances all came together to show us a Christianity on the move. Knowing this should encourage us to pray that God will do something unlikely *with* and *for* each of us. Who knows what adventures of faith may lie ahead of us as we commit our lives to the Lord and pray "without ceasing" for His guidance.

Lord, help me never forget that You welcome even the most unlikely people—including me—to Your family. May I in turn welcome those who might seem unlikely to me. AMEN.

INSPIRATION FROM THE BOOK OF ACTS

Now an angel of the Lord said to Philip, "Go south to the road—the desert road—that goes down from Jerusalem to Gaza." . . . and on his way he met an Ethiopian eunuch, an important official in charge of all the treasury of the Kandake (which means "queen of the Ethiopians"). This man had gone to Jerusalem to worship. . . . The Spirit told Philip, "Go to that chariot and stay near it."

—Acts 8:26–27, 29, NIV

People often say how wonderful it is to be self-employed because you're your own boss. Personally, I find being a self-employed writer difficult because—I'm my own boss. Besides all the hours I spend on writing, marketing, business correspondence, education, and record-keeping, I also put in a lot of time wondering what I should be doing. My mind flits between projects and ideas, unsure of which one to pursue. Sometimes I'm overwhelmed by the staggering number of available opportunities and resources. I often wish God would put sticky notes on my computer each day, outlining how I should arrange my schedule.

Maybe that's why I love passages in the Bible when a person receives specific instructions. As the early apostles worked to spread the good news about Jesus, God directed Philip to take the road toward Gaza. Philip's obedience led him to the right place and the right person at just the right time. The eunuch was reading a passage of Scripture, and once Philip explained its meaning, the man became a Christ follower. He joyfully returned home, carrying the gospel with him.

We may or may not receive specific instructions regarding life decisions, but the Lord does tell us which direction to go. When He called His first disciples, He told them, "Follow me" (John 1:43, NIV). As long as we're doing our best to follow His will, we'll always find ourselves in the right place at the right time.

—*Dianne Neal Matthews*

Notes

Notes

LESSON 4: ACTS 13:1–15:35

Establishing the Pattern

Savior, help me to establish only those patterns in my life that glorify and please You. Amen.

Keeping in mind the outline that Acts 1:8 (NIV) provides for us—"you will be my witnesses in Jerusalem [1], and in all Judea and Samaria [2], and to the ends of the earth [3]"—we are now entering the third major division of that commission. The faith has been established in Jerusalem and in Judea and Samaria. From this point on we will see how it develops "to the ends of the earth." And in this lesson we will examine the establishment of the basic apostolic pattern for expanding the outreach of the Christian gospel through the story of Paul's first missionary journey.

Paul's First Missionary Journey (13–14)

The Sending Church

At the very beginning of our lesson (13:1–3), Luke makes it plain that the basis for Christian outreach is the local congregation of believers. And behind every individual witnessing outreach is the presence of a praying and supporting group. The church at Antioch of Syria was just such a church. As we read the opening verses of our Scripture lesson, it isn't the least bit surprising that God chose this vigorous congregation to launch Christ's mission into all the world. Luke writes: "While they were worshiping the Lord and fasting, the Holy Spirit said, 'Set apart for me Barnabas and Saul for the work to which I have called them.' Then after fasting and praying they laid their hands on them and sent them off" (13:2–3, NIV).

It will help us in our own growth and spiritual development to take a close look at the character of those Antioch Christians and the qualities of the church that set apart and sponsored the first missionary efforts of Paul and Barnabas.

First, the church was made up of a reputable congregation of believers. Remember, Antioch of Syria was a bustling, pagan metropolis, but it was here that the title "Christian" was given to followers of Christ. The genuineness of their faith and life showed that they had been with Jesus. From that base of solid believability, the world outreach of Christianity could grow.

It is amazing how interconnected our witness and our reputations are. If as Christians our words and our actions don't match, our influence and our witness become tarnished and not believable. This is true in the neighborhoods and towns in which we live, and it is equally true on a national and international scale. To have power, our witness must be reputable and our behavior unimpeachable.

A second quality that distinguished the Antioch church was its diverse congregation. The believers were involved with a diversity of ministries. Two ministries are mentioned especially in verse 1: prophecy and teaching. Teachers were involved in training and nurturing their fellow Christians in the churches. On the other hand, the prophets traveled across the countryside preaching God's Word and seeking converts. It was this diversity of gifts and abilities that enabled them to be effective Christians.

We notice also that they were racially diverse. Five persons who were apparently in leadership positions are mentioned (13:1). Simeon called Niger was probably Black and from Africa, and Lucius was from Cyrene, also in Africa. Saul was, of course, a Jew from Tarsus in Cilicia, and Barnabas was a Jew from Cyprus, with the fifth being someone named Manaen, "who had been brought up with Herod the tetrarch" (NIV.) It seems clear from this brief mention that neither race nor geographical location was a barrier to inclusion or leadership in the church of Antioch. This in itself certainly set an international mood so important to a missionary vision.

While we know little about some of these men, it is likely that the church was quite socioeconomically diverse. It seems likely that Barnabas and Simeon were not persons of high social standing. On the other hand, Manaen apparently had connections in high social and political circles because of Luke's careful mention of his connection with Herod. And we have every reason to believe that Paul's family was prominent in Tarsus. Just this brief mention would seem to indicate both a socially diverse and a socially inclusive congregation. There is a vitality to this kind of atmosphere that is lacking when everyone in any group seems to be cut from the same mold. The Christians in Antioch had their priorities straight—they weren't going out to establish churches with any particular kind of social ranking. Their vision was to expand the body of Christ.

And finally, we know that the Antioch church had a worshipful congregation (13:2–3). They fasted and prayed, and it was in this attitude of worship that the Lord was able to speak to them about Barnabas and Paul. We can only speculate as to whether or not this call would or could have come had they not been devoted to worship, prayer, and fasting, but it seems improbable. How many Christians and churches miss their "word from the Lord" because they are not committed to worship?

We know, too, that at Antioch worship was not perfunctory, for Luke says, "they were serving the Lord" (verse 2, NASB). The word *serving* in Greek expresses *performing ministry to* the Lord. In other words, when they worshipped God, their worship was not a passive act; it required instead an active involvement.

This brings us now to the fourth quality that distinguished the church at Antioch. They were a *responsive* group of Christians. Paul and Barnabas had been central figures in the founding of the church. Consequently, it would have been easy for the members to want to keep them there in ongoing leadership. This is our attitude so often. We tend to focus on the capabilities and personality of the pastor—everything is planned and built around him or her. But at Antioch it was different. They didn't identify the life of their church with any person or group. They were not locked into any person for success. This gave them the freedom to openly respond to God's voice when He spoke to them.

There is so much for us to reflect upon in the opening three verses of this lesson, and we can learn a great deal from these first-century Syrian Christians. They have given us a model of integrity in words and actions, a pattern for unity in diversity, and an awareness of the vitality of worship.

Beyond Magic

Following their commissioning by the Antioch Christians, Paul and Barnabas, accompanied by young John Mark, took a ship at Seleucia, the seaport for Antioch, and sailed to Cyprus, Barnabas's homeland. Their first stop was at the port city of Salamis on the east end of the island (13:5). After delivering their message of Good News there, they traveled west across the rugged country to Paphos, a seaport city at the west end of the island and headquarters for the Roman government there. Here, two interesting characters enter the scene: Sergius Paulus, the Roman proconsul, and a magician named Elymas (13:5–12).

As the drama unfolds, it becomes clear that Sergius Paulus was open to the gospel message, even though Paphos, as a city, was devoted to the worship of Venus. But Elymas the magician (also described in verse 6 as a "false prophet") attempted to divert the proconsul's interest. He knew that if Sergius Paulus became a Christian, his influence as a magician or sorcerer would be over. Out of the many things that happened on Cyprus, Luke chose to highlight this event. We can only speculate what his reason was, but more than likely he wanted to build a case against the evil and destructive deception involved in the kind of magic Elymas practiced.

When we speak of magic here, we're not referring to the harmless sleight-of-hand tricks and illusions that are performed for the amusement of an audience. Elymas practiced a sinister kind of magic and fortune-telling, one that perverted "the right ways of the Lord" (13:10, KJV). In effect, Elymas had Sergius Paulus "under his spell," and, of course, anything that would remove that spell was a threat.

Paul, Luke tells us, was equal to the test and, inspired by the Holy Spirit, castigated Elymas publicly and declared that he would be blind for a time (13:10–11). When Sergius Paulus saw the power of the Holy Spirit acting through Paul, he became a believer in Jesus Christ.

How do we apply this episode to our own lives? In this episode we have an object lesson on the necessity of moving beyond any and all false illusions that can blind us to reality. We are to move beyond reliance on self or dependency on anything or anyone. Any dependency—except on God—is an illusion that is tragically deceptive.

We live in a time of wonders. If our great-great-grandparents could visit our world today, they would think they had stepped into a magic kingdom—telephones that we carry in our pockets and let us see each other in bright, crisp color when we talk, TVs the size of theater screens, information of all sorts available in an instant, space travel, organ transplants, effective treatments they could only imagine for illnesses of all kinds . . . In all the wonders of modern life there is the subtle temptation to give in to the illusion of being our own gods. But the message of Paul and Barnabas and John Mark on Cyprus a little over 2,000 years ago, that only through Jesus Christ do we find reality and meaning, is our up-to-date answer for today.

Beyond Tradition

The move beyond magic takes us past the limits of secularized worldviews about the meaning of life. The move beyond tradition, which we will consider now, transcends the limits of religion, narrowly understood. This section of Acts (13:13–52) pictures graphically how difficult that is. Just as Elymas opposed the move beyond magic, the Jews in Pisidian Antioch opposed the move beyond tradition.

Author and Christian martyr Dietrich Bonhoeffer was one of the first theologians to speak of "religionless Christianity." He was calling for the church to move beyond the limits of its perspective (no matter how well-intentioned or sincerely held) to embrace a bigger view of Christianity than ever before. This is precisely what Paul and Barnabas were doing when they moved into Antioch in Pisidia.

Before going on, though, let's pick up on their travels. When their mission in Paphos on Cyprus was completed, the three travelers sailed northwest to Perga in the province of Pamphylia, located on the south coast of Asia Minor. It was here that John Mark abruptly left Paul and Barnabas and headed for home. We don't know what went wrong, but we do know there was ill feeling because of what happened at the beginning of Paul's second missionary journey.

From the port city of Perga, Paul and Barnabas set out for Antioch in Pisidia. Their journey of approximately 160 miles called for them to make their way over rugged country from sea level to an altitude of over 3,500 feet to Antioch on the other side of the Taurus Mountains. It is likely they arrived there in the late summer of AD 45–46.

The scene in Antioch opens with Paul and Barnabas in the synagogue, where, after the reading of the Scriptures, they were invited to speak. The scene continues then to the next Sabbath day, when crowds gathered in huge numbers to hear Paul again, and the Jewish leaders became envious of their popularity. We see in this part of our lesson that the *move beyond tradition is first from within* (13:13–46). In the major part of this section Luke gives us Paul's address that first Sabbath day in the synagogue. Here we have a marvelous example of his preaching.

In the sermon, we see how Paul attempts to move his listeners beyond their tradition from within it. He traces how God had "moved" the Jews along from the time of their being chosen by God as His special people, throughout their 400 years of slavery and oppression in Egypt, their exodus and years in the wilderness, to their entry into the promised land. He then shows how God had "moved" them from being led by judges and prophets to being ruled by kings. And he climaxes his sermon by indicating that King David himself pointed to the coming of Jesus Christ. Paul had given them an excellent lesson on their religious roots, and it was evidently well received.

Such reviews of our faith are helpful, and even necessary, if we are to see things in perspective and get a vision for the next step in our Christian development. This is why so many of the teachings and sermons found in our Bible include the recounting of past events. A "memory" of the past is essential to understanding both the present and the future. As we "connect" with our tradition, we are given a sense of continuity with the actions of God in times past. And at the same time, we are better able to understand the present implications of our tradition.

We could all benefit from a thoughtful recollection and examination of our own Christian tradition. An understanding of where we are and where we came from will position us in a community of believers in which we are comfortable and feel at home. And we may discover aspects of our background and tradition that will move us beyond where we are now even as we remain true to our heritage. This can be a very exciting pilgrimage toward Christian maturity.

Paul's message was clear that day in the synagogue. Everything within the tradition of his listeners focused on the coming of Jesus Christ and culminated in His death and resurrection. We find a marked similarity between Paul's sermon here and that of Peter on the Day of Pentecost (Acts 2). The challenge is to build on the past, acknowledge that Jesus Christ was the fulfillment of their history, and move ahead into the future under the leadership of the Holy Spirit.

We come now to that second Sabbath day in Antioch. While large crowds gathered to hear Paul, the Jewish leaders, envious of his popularity, began to spread dissension and accused him of blasphemy. It was then that Paul exploded a bombshell with the word that the move beyond tradition is not only from within but *from without* (13:46–52). They had to believe that God was just as willing to offer Christ to the Gentile as to the Jew. And Paul made it clear that their instructions from the Lord were to be "a light for the Gentiles, that you may bring salvation to the ends of the earth" (13:47, ESV). Naturally, when the Gentiles in the crowd heard this, they were delighted and many believed, but the Jews were angry and incited the crowd to opposition and persecution.

The *move from without* in this case called for the Jew to accept the Gentile. It leads us to a spirit of mutual love and cooperation with our Christian brothers and sisters who are a part of traditions that differ from ours. Our tendency to be critical of any and all who don't dot the *i* and cross the *t* just the way we do goes against the prayer of Jesus for unity in John 17. Later Paul expressed it well when he wrote, "There is neither Jew nor Gentile, neither slave nor free, nor is there male and female, for you are all one in Christ Jesus" (Galatians 3:28, NIV). The gospel flame had been lit. It had spread from Jerusalem into Judea and Samaria. Now it had cut a path into the heart of Asia Minor—Pisidian Antioch in what is now central Turkey.

Beyond Praise and Persecution

When Paul and Barnabas moved out on this first missionary journey, they had no idea what the response to their efforts would be. They knew what we must know—there are no guarantees. Chapter 14 of Acts shows us that we must move beyond a dependence on praise or fear of persecution in our life and service to God.

When Paul and Barnabas left Antioch, they traveled southeast about 90 miles on the Roman road to the ancient city of Iconium. Here as before, the two missionaries boldly proclaimed the message of salvation (14:1), and while many believed, those who did not set out to make trouble. Paul and Barnabas nevertheless stood firm, and it is thought that they stayed on in Iconium for the entire winter.

Remaining in Iconium despite opposition and persecution was a vital necessity for the confirmation of the new believers. Paul and Barnabas knew that the new Christians were far from established in their faith. Had the missionaries not stuck by them, these new believers might have been lost to the opposition. This is an important truth for us to remember in our own experience. Our task is not only to point others to Christ but also to stand by them and with them as they move toward maturity. We need to be cautious about hit-and-run witnessing.

It would seem that staying in Iconium was vitally important for Paul and Barnabas in their confrontation with the paganism of the Graeco-Roman world and its sophisticated culture. This called not only for warmhearted witnessing and preaching but also for hardheaded debate. As Christianity moved into this arena, it was forced to interact with long-standing philosophical, religious, and political value systems. Only those who were prepared to become engaged in dialogue with those systems could ever hope to sway men and women from them. This is why it is important that we not withdraw or insulate ourselves from society and culture if our witness is to be understood and have credibility.

Paul and Barnabas were obviously well suited for their task. Paul's background and training both in Tarsus and in Jerusalem had ably prepared him for dialogue with the intelligentsia in the Greek and Roman world. His early training served him well as a Christian communicator. And we learn from this the importance of our being well trained for our role of living out our Christian faith in the complex world of today. Competent, trained ministers and lay persons are essential to the movement of the Good News into our world. This is precisely why the kind of Bible study we're involved in here is so important: as we know and understand our faith, we become better witnesses for the Lord.

But, finally, the opposition in Iconium became too strong. The mobs got violent and threatened a lynching, so Paul and Barnabas traveled southwest from Iconium to Lystra, about a six-hour trip. Luke then explains that they preached the gospel there, in nearby Derbe and the surrounding area. It was here that Paul and Barnabas confronted a different kind of problem (14:8–18). And in this episode we learn that the basis for our service to the Lord is not in *praise* received.

When Paul healed the man in Lystra who had never been able to walk, he unwittingly unleashed a wave of emotion that soon got out of hand. The people of Lystra were immersed in Roman and Greek mythology, and they immediately interpreted the healing as being done by Jupiter and Mercurius, known as Zeus and Hermes in Greek lore (14:12). Luke then tells us that the priest of Jupiter made preparation to offer sacrifices to them (14:13). It is significant that Paul and Barnabas stood as firmly against this false praise as they had against the fierce persecution in Iconium.

Paul's reaction to what had happened is interesting. Luke writes that he and Barnabas tore their clothes and ran around among the people, shouting, "We also are men, of like nature with you" (14:15, ESV). They tried desperately to show their humanity. Their confidence in the gospel was so great that they knew this exposure of their humanness would not detract from it.

Paul and Barnabas were realists. Their actions here remind us that real people are Christ's best witnesses. The Incarnation of Jesus reminds us that humanity is an acceptable "package" for transmitting the gospel message. And when we realize that, we are free to do what Paul and Barnabas did—concentrate on the message, not on ourselves (14:15–17).

And it is the message that Jesus Christ came to give us new life that counts. It isn't the personality or the looks of the messenger that makes the difference. Religious sideshows are not the vehicle for relieving the hurts of people. There's no need to jazz up the message. It's as simple now as it was in the first century: "Yet to all who did receive him, to those who believed in his name, he gave the right to become children of God" (John 1:12, NIV).

The "high" soon became a low. Some Jews from Antioch and Iconium had possibly heard about what was happening in Lystra. After hurrying there, they were successful in turning the people against Paul. Their former adulation turned to hatred. They stoned Paul and left him for dead. But Luke tells us he wasn't dead, and when he revived, he courageously went right back into the city and spent the night there before going on to Derbe (14:20).

After preaching and witnessing in Derbe, Paul and Barnabas then retraced their steps—going first to Lystra, then to Iconium and Antioch. At each stage of the trip, they affirmed and encouraged the new Christians who had found the Lord during the missionaries' earlier visit. Finally, they moved south to Perga and then over to Attalia, where they took a ship back to Antioch in Syria.

The time involved in this first missionary journey is an estimated three years. The gospel of Jesus had now moved into several Roman outposts in Asia Minor in its march toward the imperial city itself. And throughout the entire trip, Paul and Barnabas had remained faithful to their calling despite both persecution and unwarranted praise. They had risked much as they sought new converts and nurtured new Christians. The cost had been high, but as Dietrich Bonhoeffer expressed it, "When Christ calls a man, he bids him come and die."

The Jerusalem Council (15:1–35)

The Winchester Mystery House in San Jose, California, is a regular stop for tour buses. Many years ago, as the story goes, Mrs. Sarah Winchester, the wealthy, eccentric widow of the gun manufacturer William Winchester, had the peculiar notion that she wouldn't die as long as she kept building on and adding rooms to her house. Rooms were added willy-nilly, and to the rooms were added fake passageways and false staircases. Naturally, the house lacks continuity, design, and focus. It serves as a grim reminder of what can happen when reality is exchanged for fanaticism.

In our study of Acts so far we have observed a church growing rapidly and in diverse settings. If we could step back and view the scene from a distance, we might see something akin to the Winchester Mystery House. The close-up design might not seem cohesive, and certainly, the rapid growth was not without its problems.

Trouble in Antioch

When Paul and Barnabas returned to the church in Antioch, Syria, they found it in turmoil. A deputation of Jewish Christians had arrived there from Judea and had declared, "Unless you are circumcised according to the custom of Moses, you cannot be saved" (15:1, NASB). In other words, the Gentile Christians had to become Jews or they couldn't be saved. Obviously, these Jerusalem Jews were among those who viewed Christianity as nothing more than a Jewish sect. Old ways of thinking and believing die hard—certainly some beliefs had not died at all.

So, with the grand success of their first missionary tour just barely behind them, Paul and Barnabas and the rest of the Christians in Antioch had to wrestle with their most critical problem yet. When the issue couldn't be settled locally, "Paul and Barnabas and some of the others were appointed to go up to Jerusalem to the apostles and the elders about this question" (15:2, ESV). The question was critical: Was the gospel only for the Jews or was it for everyone?

And so we have the setting for what has since been referred to as the First Church Council or the Apostolic Council, which met in Jerusalem in AD 49.

The Council in Session

The apostles and elders gathered in a formal meeting. Of primary importance is that they started off by allowing *a full airing of opinion.* Earlier Paul and Barnabas had given a full report on their trip and on the dispute in Antioch. Then Peter, having learned his lesson well in Joppa and Caesarea, argued against the attempt to Judaize the Gentile Christians (15:7–11). Next Paul and Barnabas spoke to the assembly, "declaring what miracles and wonders God had wrought among the Gentiles by them" (15:12, KJV).

There seems to have been no limit placed on the debate. No perspective was given preference over another during the discussion. Also, no assumptions about right and wrong were made prematurely. Everyone involved was a Christian, and all the participants were allowed to speak. The atmosphere was charged because of the importance of the issue.

Following the discussion, the group *looked to trusted leaders to bring perspective.* Then after Peter, Paul, and Barnabas were heard, James, the acknowledged leader of the church in Jerusalem, spoke (15:13–21). The atmosphere was one of quiet and respectful attentiveness. The issue was momentous.

As James spoke, it became clear that *the Scriptures were the final court of appeal.* Even though the witness of the respected apostles seemed conclusive, no decision was made without confirmation from the Old Testament. The prophecy of Amos (9:11–12) served as the ultimate voice. Through it the prophet spoke of the restoration of Israel, but did so not in terms of the Jews alone but also of the Gentiles.

The sequence of events in this meeting is impressive. First, all opinions were heard. Then came the perspective of the mature leaders, and under the guidance of James the authority of the Scriptures was invoked. Finally, James offered the solution. The Gentile Christians would not be required to adhere to the traditions of Judaism. But in order to make it possible for Jew and Gentile to experience fellowship together without social strain, the Gentiles were asked to avoid idol contamination of any kind, to not practice fornication, and to eat nothing that had been strangled and from which the blood had not been drained (in other words, their meat was to be prepared according to Jewish custom). By reaching these compromises and following these simple rules, Jew and

Gentile Christians could associate together without offending each other.

Antioch Christians Reassured

Now we come to the final act in the Church Council drama. *The decision was clearly communicated* (15:22–31). It was to be written down carefully and entrusted to Judas and Silas, who were to accompany Paul and Barnabas and deliver it in person to the Christians in Syrian Antioch. The key words here are "it has seemed good to the Holy Spirit and to us" (15:28, ESV). Here we see the coming together of divine and human wills. That alone could have produced the spirit of "one accord" (15:25, KJV), which ultimately came to characterize the Jerusalem conference.

Behind all of this is an unspoken but significant fact: there is no mention that anyone was excommunicated from the fellowship. People on both sides of the dispute still appeared to be in the church after the smoke had cleared away. This in itself is a powerful testimony, especially when so many of our disputes today end in division, hard feelings, and members of the "losing side" leaving the church. Too often we start with division and end with schism, but they started with division and ended with unity. We forget too easily that the purpose of decision-making is to strengthen the unity of the church. The early Christians seem to have kept the desire for unity uppermost in the whole process. The final result was a general spirit of encouragement and an underlying spirit of revival (15:31–35).

An interesting "full circle" has occurred in this lesson. We started in Antioch in Syria, and we end there. The church that contained the qualities necessary to be a sending church was also the church that had the qualities necessary to receive and integrate a critical decision. In between the basic pattern in the establishment of the Christian faith was the repeated call of God to "move beyond" those things that would have perpetually hindered the Christians.

There are many questions for us in this lesson. Are we the kind of church that can both send out the gospel in mission and receive it in decision? Have we moved beyond magic, tradition, praise, and persecution? Have we cultivated mature and respected leaders to whom we can look for perspective? Do we accept the Bible as normative in matters of faith and practice, and do we know it well enough to be able to distinguish between a word from the Lord and a proof text?

These are all vital questions to us now, even as they were to first-century Christians. We've come a long way since then, but the principles illuminated in this lesson are still valid today.

Lord, help me follow the example of the Christians in the first church council in my relationships with fellow believers. May our fellowship always come from a spirit of unity and cooperation. AMEN.

INSPIRATION FROM THE BOOK OF ACTS

He has shown kindness by giving you rain from heaven and crops in their seasons; he provides you with plenty of food and fills your hearts with joy.

—Acts 14:17, NIV

I was not having fun. Our one apple tree was abundant with fruit, and as I did not have time for pies or applesauce, I tossed the apples into a plastic pail to pour over the back fence. It was the fourth time for cleanup duty.

But as I lifted the first bucket over, I saw I had company. Seven deer stood frozen a dozen feet away. They had been feasting on last week's apple bounty, and even though I backed up, they leaped away.

Then I had an idea. Now that they knew where dinner was, perhaps they would hop the fence and clean up the rotting mess for me.

I was right. The next morning, I saw the deer in our backyard. After a six-foot leap over the fence, they were feasting on the fruit. But then one strolled toward my flower bed. Hmm, that was enough. I opened the door, and one by one they scampered away.

Over the coming weeks, the deer and I seemingly came to an arrangement. I allowed them space, and they stayed away from my flowers. It was a great exchange, saving me time and backaches.

God provides for all our needs. Earlier in our marriage when we were waiting out payday, an extra check would show up. Often when I was too exhausted after a full day of teaching, I'd find my friend's warm pot roast on my counter. If I couldn't shuttle one of our four kids to a game, another parent was happy to help.

In the Old Testament, one name the Hebrews had for God was Jehovah Jireh. It means "God provides." And yes, indeed, He does.

—Janet Holm McHenry

Notes

Notes

LESSON 5: ACTS 15:36–18:22

Responding to the Unexpected: Paul's Second Missionary Journey

Redeemer, open my eyes, my ears, my heart, to receive the truths You have for me in this lesson. AMEN.

One of the greatest testing times in our faith comes when we are confronted by the unexpected. When life falls into neat, predictable patterns, we easily develop a sense of confidence and even control over our lives. However, to do this is to live under an illusion. In fact, life is always unpredictable. We constantly live on the edge of the unexpected and the unknown. How we think and function when we cross over that edge is a matter of great importance in our discipleship.

In this lesson we will watch Paul experience and respond to many unexpected events in his life and ministry. As the lesson opens, it is clear that his intention was to pay a comfortable follow-up visit to those he had previously won and nurtured in the faith (15:36). That decision in itself, plus the events that transpired, brings "the unexpected" clearly into focus.

From Antioch to Troas (15:36–16:10)

Problems with Partners

As soon as the Jerusalem Council adjourned, Paul and Barnabas traveled the almost 400 miles north to Antioch to report the results. And it was here that they faced a great personal crisis. What seemed like the period of greatest unity for them turned out to be their time of greatest disunity.

As they prepared to embark on their second missionary journey to revisit the churches they had earlier established in Asia Minor, Barnabas wanted to take his nephew John Mark along. Paul refused and they went separate ways, never to labor together again (15:37–41).

Here is probably the most ironic event in the book of Acts. Barnabas was the central figure in Paul's acceptance by the church after his conversion. Together they formed the "winning combination" in establishing Christianity in the key cities of Syria and Asia Minor. Working in harmony, they had helped overcome a potentially destructive controversy in the church at the Jerusalem council. If ever there was a "team" in the Christian faith, Paul and Barnabas were it. Yet their difference of opinion was so strong now that they separated. What does this say to us?

First, it warns us of the danger of living by assumption. John Mark's defection on that first trip didn't seem to have created much controversy at the time it happened (13:13). Perhaps Paul and Barnabas both assumed they had worked through the issue. But ironically, it became the very thing that led to their separation. And in comparison to other events and issues they'd faced, it seemed to be a little thing. But it was the issue now that threatened to disrupt God's work. This happens all too often in our churches today. Frequently, when things appear to be going smoothly, contention and disunity create problems.

Second, it warns us that spiritual victory does not insulate us from spiritual chaos. The church at Antioch was just completing one of its greatest periods of encouragement and revival. Positive attitudes had combined with a spirit of unity to make that period a great time to be a member of that church. Yet two of their leaders were involved in a dispute. And undoubtedly this caused concern among the believers there. From our vantage point, it is difficult to make a judgment as to who was right or wrong in this case. We do know, though, that in times of intense disagreement and contention among Christians, a spirit of division and distrust can easily move in and create havoc.

Third, it reminds us that what may appear to be an initial defeat does not necessarily undo the will of God. Fortunately, this did not happen in this instance. Barnabas took John Mark and returned to Cyprus (15:39). And we have no reason to believe that Barnabas had anything other than a successful ministry on this and subsequent missionary trips. We do know from later references that apparently Barnabas's faith in Mark was justified. And there was even an apparent reconciliation between Paul and Mark, for in 2 Timothy, Paul wrote, "Luke alone is with me. Get Mark and bring him with you, for he is very useful to me for ministry" (2 Timothy 4:11, ESV).

Paul and Silas Revisit the Churches

As we move through this lesson—the account of Paul's second missionary journey—we will see that God blessed his efforts greatly and dramatically. From Antioch Paul and Silas headed north on foot almost 150 miles to Tarsus. And from there they made their way through the rugged and steep pass known as the Cilician Gates that cut across the 7,000-foot-high Taurus Mountains. Next, they moved west to Derbe and Lystra—probably some 125 to 150 miles from Tarsus. Here Paul and Silas connected with Timothy, a promising young man.

Paul was quite taken with Timothy and selected him as a traveling companion in the Lord. But first Luke tells us that Paul "took him and circumcised him because of the Jews who were in those parts, for they all knew that his father was a Greek" (16:3, NASB). On the surface Paul's action here may seem confusing. After all, hadn't the Jerusalem council settled the entire matter of circumcision?

Yes, it had, but we need to remember that the Jerusalem ruling applied to the Gentiles. Timothy was half Jewish. And so the circumcision of Timothy was a witness to two powerful truths, both of which were vitally important in Paul's ministry and to the development of the Christian faith.

First, Paul acknowledged Timothy's Jewishness in the act of circumcision and thus legitimized the marriage of his Jewish mother to his Greek father. To the strict Jew this marriage would not have been valid. By circumcising Timothy, Paul demonstrated that he had risen above the narrow interpretation of the Law and that he accepted Timothy's parents now as full participants in God's covenant.

Second, Paul acknowledged the need to fully integrate Timothy into the heritage of his Jewishness. Had Timothy been a full-blooded Gentile, Paul would not have circumcised him. But because he was partly Jewish, Paul did not want any occasion to arise among fellow Jews where Timothy's personhood would be questioned.

We might well ask ourselves at this point: what are the practical lessons in all of this? There are at least two. First, Paul was completely freed from racial and nationalistic barriers in the expression of the Christian faith—the gospel was indeed for all. At the same time, he remained sensitive to the traditions of Jewish life and thought. It is terribly easy for us to become paternalistic and nationalistic in our interpretation of Christianity. But we have in Paul's actions here a model of Christian behavior that rises above human-imposed barriers and is still sensitive to the feelings of others.

The second thing is the importance of a nurturing ministry. Our calling is to be Christian mentors to those around us. In Timothy, Paul saw a promising young person, and he set out to build the young man up in the faith.

Before continuing, let's take a moment to examine an interesting thing that has happened here. Paul established the prototype of team ministry on his first missionary journey. With him on that journey were Barnabas and young John Mark. That combination would no longer work. But Paul still apparently believed in team ministry because he now had Silas and young Timothy with him—two people who were to remain close to him for the rest of his life.

Now Luke picks up in the action (16:6–8). The details are sparse, but we know that the three men traveled "through the region of Phrygia and Galatia, having been forbidden by the Holy Spirit to speak the word in Asia. And when they had come up to Mysia, they attempted to go into Bithynia, but the Spirit of Jesus did not allow them. So, passing by Mysia, they went down to Troas" (ESV). This simply means that from Derbe and Lystra, they traveled on to Iconium and Pisidian Antioch and from there headed north and west to Troas (near ancient Troy) on the Aegean seacoast—an overland trip of about 900 miles, probably all covered on foot. This is a long trip across modern Turkey in an automobile. On foot, it must have been a grueling and hazardous journey!

When God Says No

Before moving into the dramatic event at Troas, let's reflect for a moment on another aspect of this lesson. Everything that is written about Paul suggests that he was a man of careful planning. This second missionary trip began with the clear intention of visiting the Christians and the churches where he had been before (15:36). And in the early phases of the trip, everything seemed to move along according to plan.

After a time, though, it seems that Paul wanted to take the gospel into a new territory. He wanted to travel to the far northern parts of Asia Minor. Had he done this it would have meant that the Christian gospel would have penetrated as far north as the Black Sea. But Luke tells us that on two occasions his plans were redirected by the Holy Spirit (16:6–7). Instead, Paul was directed west to Troas.

This raises the interesting question of how we should respond when God says no to us and our plans. Most of us have had the experience of making plans that we felt sure were right, but then something happened that moved us in a different direction. And because of this, there are three reasons why this particular experience of Paul's can be helpful to us.

First, there is nothing about this experience that *belittles the fact that Paul had made plans for a certain course of action.* In a very matter-of-fact manner Luke paints a picture for us here of a divinely appointed missionary who tried to do the right thing. I'm sure he had prayed and asked to know God's will for him and his party. And once he felt he had it, he acted. While He might correct our plans, God never belittles a person who acts according to the guidance he or she feels has been given.

Second, this part of the lesson makes it clear that *God is sovereign, and we are to remain flexible as we move ahead with our plans.* We don't get any hint in the words of Acts 16:6–8 that Paul and his party were uptight or frustrated. Instead, we see the guidance of the Holy Spirit at work and their acceptance of what was happening. We don't see any indication that Paul tried to force his will on God or manipulate circumstances to get his way.

Third, *we are reminded that God's* no *will lead us to a better* yes. At first, Paul's vision had been to cover a small territory, but now in Troas he receives a vision for eastern Europe (16:8–10). God speaks to him through a vision, and he sees a man from Macedonia who says, "Come over into Macedonia, and help us" (16:9, KJV). This was clearly the voice of God—His no to northern Asia Minor was a yes to Europe.

The Gospel in Greece (16:11–18:17)

Heeding the Call

It was at Troas that Luke joined Paul and Silas and Timothy. There is an interesting shift of pronouns from "they" to "we" in verse 10: "After Paul had seen the vision, *we* got ready at once to leave for Macedonia, concluding that God had called *us* to preach the gospel to them" (NIV, italics added for emphasis). The four men then took a ship, in obedience to the vision, and sailed across the northern part of the Aegean Sea to the port city of Neapolis—modern-day Kavala, Greece—a distance of almost 150 miles. And from there they walked inland on the Roman Egnatian Way 15 miles to the city of Philippi. Philippi was an old and established Roman colony, heavily populated by retired Roman soldiers and their families. Here Paul was to establish his first foothold for the Lord in Europe. Here, too, he was brought into contact with a wide variety of people. Some would respond readily; others would be difficult and contentious. This would be true throughout the entire trip, but Paul's training up to this point had prepared him well.

The First Convert at Philippi

There were so few Jews in Philippi that there wasn't a synagogue. So on the Sabbath Paul and his companions went down to the river where some godly inclined people evidently met together. There they met "a woman named Lydia . . . she was a seller of purple fabrics from the city of Thyatira, and a worshipper of God" (16:14, NASB). Luke then tells us that she heard Paul's message, was converted, and opened up her home for them to use as their headquarters in Philippi (16:13–15). Luke carefully identifies Lydia with her hometown of Thyatira, a Roman colony in the province of Asia about 100 miles southeast of Troas. It is possible that sometime after this, Lydia returned to Thyatira and was one of the founders of the church there.

One of the great joys of Christianity is that it brings us into fellowship with some marvelous people—people who, like Lydia, use hospitality as an effective form of evangelism. It is quite possible that her practice of hospitality was contagious among the growing Christian community of Philippi, because some ten years after this first visit of Paul's to Philippi, he wrote to them and said, "I thank my God in all my remembrance of you, always in every prayer of mine for you all making my prayer with joy, because of your partnership in the gospel from the first day until now" (Philippians 1:3–5, ESV). Friendly hospitality is a powerful form of Christian witness!

Paul and Silas Arrested

The scene shifts drastically now from Lydia to a enslaved girl with a "spirit of divination" (16:16, KJV). Her apparent ability to tell fortunes was exploited by her masters. The girl followed Paul and his fellow missionaries around, "crying out, 'These men are servants of the Most High God, who proclaim to you the way of salvation'" (Acts 16:17, ESV). When Paul commanded the spirit to come out of her in the name of Jesus Christ and she was healed, her masters were furious and charged Paul and Silas with disturbing the peace and being troublemakers. Since the Roman authorities prided themselves on their ability to maintain order, anyone accused of causing trouble and of being a public nuisance was dealt with severely. Paul and Silas were arrested and beaten. They were then put in chains and thrown into jail.

The drama now moves toward its climax. Paul and Silas didn't act like flogged prisoners—they prayed and sang praises unto God. And at midnight, Luke tells us, there was "such a violent earthquake that the foundations of the prison were shaken. At once all the prison doors flew open, and everyone's chains came loose" (16:25–26, NIV).

The Conversion of the Jailer

The jailer was jolted to consciousness by the earthquake, and when he saw all the doors open, he assumed his prisoners had escaped. Rather than suffer that disgrace, he drew his sword and was about to kill himself when Paul called out and assured him that all the prisoners were still there (16:27–28). First, in verse 25 when Paul and Silas were singing and praying, Luke tells us the other prisoners "were listening to" them (verse 25, ESV). The Greek word Luke used here is not a common one, and it is a strong verb—it means "listening eagerly or attentively." Now the terrified jailer *heard* Paul's words of reassurance and was apparently so awed by what had happened that he asked the crucial question, "Sirs, what must I do to be saved?" (verse 30, KJV). Back came the answer that has shaken the world from then until now: "Believe in the Lord Jesus, and you will be saved—you and your household" (verse 31, NIV).

The jailer believed. And we know this not just from what Luke tells us but from what the jailer did next. He bathed their wounds and fed them. Frequently, it isn't our words that impress people but our actions. A Christian is not just a talker—but a doer. We don't know anything more about this jailer than what Luke tells us here, but it is not improbable to think that he told and retold the story of what happened to him that night.

The scene closes with the jailer telling Paul and Silas that the magistrates had released them. But Paul now advised them of the fact that he and Silas were Roman citizens and, as such, should never have been beaten, and he demanded a public apology.

Yes, like the four missionaries to Philippi, we, too, will run into all kinds of people as we move through life in our adventure of faith. Some are easy to get along with; others are difficult. But our mission as Christians is to bring healing and joy to everyone who crosses our path.

In It Together at Thessalonica

With the change of pronouns (from "we" to "they") in 17:1, it would appear that Luke stayed behind in Philippi while Paul, Silas, and Timothy set out along the Egnatian Way for the city of Thessalonica, modern Salonica. Luke dismisses the trip with just a few words, but it was a distance of between 85 and 100 miles. As we watch while Paul and Silas and Luke minister in both Thessalonica and Berea, we will begin to see an undercurrent of relationship between them and the new Christians, which can best be described by the Greek word *koinonia* (coy-no-NEE-uh), usually translated "fellowship" (17:1–15).

Upon arrival in Thessalonica, Paul spent three weeks teaching in the synagogue to the Jews with virtually no results except a few Gentiles who responded from the sidelines. However, Paul continued his efforts and his hearers were soon divided into two distinct categories: those who accepted his message gladly and those who didn't and wanted to cause trouble. It is in this kind of setting that we begin to get our first indication of the nature of Christian fellowship. True koinonia is based on the fact that *together we have decided to follow Jesus.* Community is usually based on common experience, and under the teaching of the missionaries, the believers in Thessalonica became a church noted for its spirit of fellowship.

Another peculiarity of fellowship seen here is that it holds up under pressure. Remember, these were new Christians, but when the unbelieving opposition set out to make trouble, Jason and his fellow Christians didn't cave in and renege—a true sign of the kind of fellowship that holds firm under severe pressure (17:6–9).

There is nothing like opposition to draw us together in a true spirit of fellowship. Amid the pressure and controversy in Thessalonica we find a most descriptive statement as to the effectiveness of the Christian faith. It was said of the missionaries and the new Christians that they "turned the world upside down" (17:6, KJV). They saw in this new Christian faith and fellowship a power that could change the world. Christianity was then, and still is, a power that can change both people's lives and the world around them.

From Thessalonica, Paul and his party moved on another 45 miles west along the Roman road to Berea (17:10). Here we see that they were received more graciously at first, and Paul had the opportunity to open up the Scriptures to them daily, and many believed (17:11–12). But so bitter had been the Jewish opposition in Thessalonica that, apparently, when they heard of Paul's success in Berea, they arrived on the scene and stirred up the people to such a frenzy that Paul had to leave. Silas and Timothy did, however, stay behind for a time to minister to the new Christians.

While we may not face the kind of opposition Paul experienced here, there is a great need for a new spirit of koinonia in our Christian fellowship today. Division and strife are all too common in today's congregations, but our strength as Christians comes in pulling together. We draw strength and a sense of purpose from one another. This doesn't mean that we will all think alike or worship alike or act alike, but it does mean that in Christ we are one—we experience a true fellowship with believers, sons and daughters of God, wherever they are.

A Reasonable Faith: Paul in Athens

It is hard not to be amazed at Paul's courage. From the time of his conversion until now, he had been virtually driven from six cities because of opposition to his ministry. And yet he pressed on relentlessly. Now he was on his way alone to Athens. It was a long trip, more than 300 miles. In a sense, all of Paul's debates and encounters were mere preludes to this first Athens event. God's redirection of his ministry was taking him to the capital of Greek culture and philosophy. As we see Paul moving toward Athens and then taking his message there in the summer of AD 51, there are four things that we should take note of.

First, *Paul was willing to go to Athens*. When Paul left Berea, Athens wasn't the only place he could have gone. But he chose to go there. After all, his call as an apostle hadn't ruled out any country, culture, or mindset. His brand of Christianity was one of initiative and penetration. While Athens was an intellectual center, it was also a hotbed of pagan worship. There were probably more statues of pagan gods in this city than Paul had seen throughout all of his travels. But he knew there were no people anywhere "unfit" for the gospel. And he was aggressive in his efforts to reach new converts even as he was anxious for Christians to get along together in unity. There was nothing elitist or exclusive about Paul's faith.

When Paul actually arrived in Athens, we catch something of his feelings as Luke writes, "He was greatly distressed to see that the city was full of idols" (17:16, NIV). And we next find him meeting and talking with people in the synagogue and in the marketplace.

Second, *Paul met them on their own turf*. He was equal to the Athenian give-and-take. Paul quickly adjusted to the discourses that dated back to the times of Socrates and entered into the lively discussions wherever they occurred. This soon brought him to the attention of the Epicureans and the Stoics (17:18). Both philosophies dated back to between 200 and around 300 BC. When their adherents heard that an advocate of a new religion had arrived in town, they were curious. They took him to the Areopagus (Mars Hill), and it was there that Paul was given the opportunity to explain his faith: "May we know what this new teaching is which you are proclaiming? For you are bringing some strange things to our ears; so we want to know what these things mean" (17:19–20, NASB). Paul, now meeting them on their own ground, appealed to them in a way that was consistent with their own philosophies. He knew those philosophers were attracted by novelty. So he proclaimed "a new doctrine"—he offered a new and better philosophy.

In speaking, Paul was respectful and courteous. He made reference to their altar to The Unknown God as a means of contact and of getting their attention. He talked their language and quoted from their writings, and then he moved in, tactfully yet boldly declaring the truth of the gospel of Christ. He offered them a better way, and that is the mission of Christianity—it is our mission today.

In practical terms Christianity is relating Christ with His transforming power to *every* part of life. This was Paul, as the philosopher, who was so effective when ministering to the intellectuals in Athens. He summarized this approach in 1 Corinthians 9:22, when he wrote, "I have become all things to all people, that by all means I might save some" (ESV). Our shared interests and other commonalities, whatever they might be, give us a base for effective witnessing.

Third, *Paul approached his listeners with general affirmation.* Paul's opening remarks on Mars Hill illustrate his affirmative ability to make contact with his listeners: "I see that in every way you are very religious" (17:22, NIV). This was obvious, for there were altars and statues of gods and goddesses throughout all of Athens, and the Parthenon, that great temple of Athena, dominated the city and the surrounding countryside from its place of prominence on the Acropolis—just above Mars Hill. In their way they were reaching out to make contact with the divine. Paul very wisely recognized this and used it as a bridge to proclaim the truth of the one God, the Creator of the universe.

Paul's example here is a good one for us. Too often in our witness to people, we either say or give the impression that "You've really messed things up" or "I can tell that you've really missed it." To condemn or act superior as if we have all the truth alienates people. It cuts them off and cuts them out and our contact is lost. Paul was too wise for this. He had earned the right to their attention.

Fourth, *Paul used the bridge to carry the greater message.* Having made contact with his listeners, Paul now shared his faith (17:24–31). From his reference to creation (17:24), which was a common ground of agreement among those philosophers, he moved them along to the truth in Jesus Christ. Following the conclusion of Paul's discourse, Luke shares with us the reaction of the crowd: "When they heard about the resurrection of the dead, some of them sneered, but others said, 'We want to hear you again on this subject'" (17:32, NIV). As would be expected, there are always those who reject outright the message of Christ, but as on Mars Hill, there are also those who readily accept it or remain open.

In the Gospels, we see again and again how sensitive Jesus was to His listeners. He talked their language, and they understood Him. In our study of Acts so far we have observed Paul's sensitivity to his hearers as well: His approach was always tailored to them. But his message of salvation through Christ was the same.

Obstacles and Opportunities: Paul in Corinth

Paul is on the move again as he leaves Athens and travels to Corinth. This great metropolis was one of the major cities in the Roman Empire at that time. It was strategically located on a narrow isthmus that separated northern and southern Greece. Corinth was a majestic city dominated by the towering Acrocorinthus, a rocky hill on which was built a fortress and Aphrodite's temple.

In this final part of our lesson now, which includes this first visit of Paul to Corinth, we will have the opportunity to see how God can turn obstacles into opportunities. We will also see how we can and should respond when the unexpected happens in our lives. Admittedly, our perspectives are limited. But certain events in our lesson now remind us that when a given situation or set of circumstances appears to be a hindrance or setback, it may become an opportunity that God can use for our growth.

When Paul arrived in Corinth, he was fortunate enough to make contact with Aquila and Priscilla, a Jewish couple who had been forced to leave Italy when Claudius had banished the Jews in AD 49 (18:2). Relocating their home must have been a traumatic experience for this couple, but they were now well settled as tentmakers. And since this was Paul's vocation, their common skills brought them together. At any rate, the persecution that forced Aquila and Priscilla to leave Italy became God's opportunity for them to meet Paul.

Paul soon settled in with Aquila and Priscilla, and Luke tells us he preached and taught in the synagogue, witnessing to the truth that Jesus was the Messiah (18:4). After a time he experienced a glad reunion with Silas and Timothy. But evidently not long after their arrival, Jewish opposition to their message became so strong and bitter that Paul said, "Your blood be on your own heads! I am innocent. From now on I will go to the Gentiles" (18:6, ESV). Once again for Paul, the obstacle of opposition became an opportunity.

Luke tells us that Paul began to minister next door to the synagogue (18:7), and it wasn't long before Crispus, the ruler of the synagogue, became a believer in Jesus. Because of this conversion, other Jews in Corinth accepted Christ, and Paul received a great affirmation from the Lord (18:9–10) that we can take for ourselves today. It was this affirmation that inspired Paul to remain in Corinth for a year and a half.

What we might think of as insignificant events in our lives may not be insignificant at all from God's perspective. You can probably remember small events in your own life that turned out to be quite important, even though you couldn't see or imagine it at the time. A job change that you didn't want yet turned out to be enjoyable and satisfying. A chance meeting with someone that led to an unexpected blessing. These kinds of events remind us that when circumstances force change on us, when big opportunities seem to disappear, God may be opening a new door. Remember, it was Paul's setback in the synagogue that led him to an even greater ministry in Corinth.

Luke gives us one more scene in Corinth before Paul starts his trip home. Gallio, the Roman proconsul, enters the scene.

It is likely he had just arrived in Corinth after having received his appointment in AD 51. Luke tells us that the Jews who opposed Paul and his teaching took this opportunity to try to get a judgment against Paul. But here we find an excellent example of Roman justice. Gallio saw through the duplicity of the Jews and doubtless had inquired into Paul's character, for Gallio threw the case out of court and ruled in Paul's favor (18:12–17).

The Journey's End (18:18–22)

From Corinth to Caesarea

Finally, the time came for Paul to leave. He took a ship and, accompanied by Aquila and Priscilla, traveled across the Aegean Sea to Ephesus. The stop there was brief, but there was still time for Paul to speak in the synagogue. Evidently, Aquila and Priscilla remained in Ephesus. But Paul continued on by ship to Caesarea and then traveled overland to Antioch in Syria.

Paul's second missionary journey had taken the best part of three years. He had traveled a little over 3,000 miles—about 1,200 on the sea and almost 1,800 on land. And, undoubtedly, the land travel was all on foot. It had been a long and hard trip, but the gospel of Christ had now taken root in Europe under the guidance of the Holy Spirit.

It has been well said that when we look into the future, our vision is blurred, but hindsight is always twenty-twenty. This lesson has illustrated that truth for us. As with Paul and the early disciples, there is an unseen Presence who guides our steps.

There is an unfelt Hand that supports us along the way and a quiet and sometimes unnoticed Voice that says, "This is the way. Walk in it." And we find inspiration in this lesson to believe that as we are obedient to God and follow His leading, He will use us in unexpected ways in the magnificent drama of life.

God, give me a Spirit that sings in even the worst of circumstances. Fill me with more of Yourself. AMEN.

INSPIRATION FROM THE BOOK OF ACTS

When they came to the border of Mysia, they tried to enter Bithynia, but the Spirit of Jesus would not allow them to.

—Acts 16:7, NIV

I was having a hard time dealing with people saying no when I asked them to help with a fundraising event for a good cause. Then a friend called me and told me that her daughter's car had been totaled by a careless driver. She was desperate for transportation to her entry-level job and didn't have any credit history to buy another one. "I'll pray that your daughter will find a reliable car," I told her.

A week later my friend excitedly told me that her daughter had qualified for a loan with a credit union and found a used car that seemed perfect! Two days later my friend called back sounding defeated. "My daughter took the car title over to the credit union, and they denied her loan. They said the title search showed that the car was salvage because it had been totaled in an accident."

"Haven't we been praying for a dependable car? This is an answer to prayer," I found myself saying to my friend. "Thankfully, the title search turned up the truth. That car had problems that couldn't be seen on the outside."

As I hung up the phone, I realized that it's natural to feel disappointed and discouraged when we get "no" answers, especially when everything we see on the outside looks exactly like what we want and need.

I sat down and started listing names of other potential volunteers I could call to help with the fundraiser, thankful that God in His infinite wisdom knows enough to sometimes say no.

—Karen Barber

Notes

Notes

LESSON 6: ACTS 18:23–20:38

Strengthening the Fellowship: Paul's Third Missionary Journey

Heavenly Father, thank You for Your joy, which is my strength. AMEN.

It is not uncommon for people in midlife to return to school to further their education. Many empty nesters return to the classroom. Retirees will sometimes take or audit classes at a local college to learn new skills or polish old ones. YouTube tutorials teach thousands of people to paint or draw, fix cars, bake bread, invest in the stock market, and more.

Behind all of this is the recognition that we cannot stand still. Either we grow or we fall prey to inertia and slip into decline. The Apostle Paul was well aware that growth was essential in the spiritual life of the new Christians in the churches he had founded and nurtured.

Our last lesson closed with Paul's return to Syrian Antioch after his second missionary journey. Now Luke writes, "After spending some time in Antioch, Paul set out from there and traveled from place to place throughout the region of Galatia and Phrygia, strengthening all the disciples" (18:23, NIV). Once again Paul is on the move as he strikes out from Antioch, heading for his home city of Tarsus. From there he makes his way over the Taurus Mountains, through the narrow and arduous Cilician Gates, and into southern Galatia. Moving west steadily, he evidently visited with and instructed groups of believers wherever he could find them.

Luke doesn't give us any detail about these visits except to indicate that Paul kept moving west into Phrygia where he continued his nurturing and teaching ministry. Paul knew that a failure to follow up would result in a loss of power and vitality among these Asia Minor Christians and churches. During this time he was preaching salvation and was also actively engaged in his own style of "continuing education."

Completing the Picture (18:23–19:10)

Luke breaks away from his narrative now and introduces a new character. By doing so he draws attention to the gaps that existed in the lives of some believers in spite of the apostle's progress. This next part of our lesson gives us two examples of how Paul labored to bring new Christians into a more complete understanding and experience of the faith.

Introducing Apollos

The first example centers on the person of Apollos. In just a few words Luke gives us an amazing portrait of this Jew from Alexandria, a city founded by Alexander the Great in 332 BC. With the passing years, this Egyptian city had become a haven for expatriated Jews. Its population in the first century was about one million, of which some 400,000 were Jews.

Alexandria was a great university center that offered rich resources of learning. In fact, it was Alexandrian scholars who gave the world the Septuagint, the oldest Greek version of the Old Testament. This was the atmosphere in which Apollos obtained his education.

In his brief biographical sketch, Luke tells us that Apollos was eloquent, was highly trained in the Scriptures, was religiously learned, was fervent in spirit, and was a good teacher (18:24–25). From Luke's glowing description, we can see that he was a paragon of religious virtue.

We meet Apollos in the ancient city of Ephesus where he was teaching and preaching in the synagogue, but Luke gives us a clue that something is missing when he says that Apollos knew "only the baptism of John" (18:25, KJV). This tells us that Apollos was a disciple of John the Baptist, and as such he followed carefully the strict rules for life and conduct that were observed by the members of the Baptist's sect. Apollos understood baptism for repentance, and he knew *about* Jesus. And what he knew he represented well and with eloquent enthusiasm, but when Aquila and Priscilla heard him, they saw that something was missing. And they knew what it was.

Like John the Baptist, Apollos called people to leave behind their former ways of thinking and living. They were to repent—turn around and head in a new direction—but the message stopped there. It told them what they should leave behind; it did not tell them what they should embrace.

Aquila and Priscilla saw that while Apollos understood about baptism for repentance, he did not know about, and he hadn't experienced, the baptism of the Holy Spirit. And while he was apparently being used by the Lord to lead people to repentance, his ministry was incomplete and lacked power. And so Luke tells us that the very wise and spiritually mature Aquila and Priscilla "took him aside and explained the way of God more accurately to him" (18:26, NASB).

Now we see something in this remarkable man that commends him even further. Not only was he a good teacher, but it would appear that he was also *teachable*. There is no hint in Luke's brief mention that he resisted the instruction of Aquila and Priscilla. After all, with all of his talent, it would have been easy for him to feel offended. With the success he had experienced so far, it would have been quite understandable for him to protest, "What do I need to be instructed about?" But instead, he quietly submitted to the guidance of these new spiritual mentors of his and entered into a whole new experience of faith. And while Luke doesn't describe what happened, he writes about the results as Apollos left Ephesus and ministered throughout southern Greece: "The brothers encouraged him and wrote to the disciples to welcome him. When he arrived, he greatly *helped those who through grace had believed, for he powerfully refuted the Jews in public, showing by the Scriptures that the Christ was Jesus*" (18:27–28, ESV, italics added for emphasis).

Now Apollos had the power to help the new Christians, and he had come, through the guidance of the Holy Spirit, to a new belief that Jesus was indeed the Christ—the Messiah.

We've spent quite a bit of time in this part of our lesson on the Apollos story, and for good reason. From the brief biographical sketch Luke gave us of Apollos, we saw that he was well educated, had a good knowledge of the Scriptures, and was a gifted leader and communicator. But that was not enough for him, and it isn't for us. We may know a lot *about* Jesus but not really *know* Him in the power of the Holy Spirit. With us, as with Apollos, the power to live a rich, fulfilled, and productive Christian life comes only through the presence of the indwelling Jesus who has become Lord as well as Savior.

Paul Begins His Ministry in Ephesus

Now we pick up again on the Apostle Paul. We left him earlier moving west through Galatia and Phrygia in Asia Minor (modern Turkey). Luke brings us together now as Paul arrives in Ephesus. You remember that he had stopped off briefly here on his way home from the second missionary journey. Undoubtedly, what Paul saw on his first brief visit convinced him that he wanted to return soon and spend more time there.

In Paul's day, Ephesus was already at least 1,000 years old. It was a magnificent city, and in Roman times it was the capital of the province of Asia. Its architecture was superb, but its most majestic building was the temple of the goddess known as Artemis by the Greeks and Diana by the Romans, which was one of the Seven Wonders of the World. Even by today's standards it was a large building—220 feet wide by 425 feet long, and it stood more than 50 feet high. The city was a center for idol worship, and the cult of Artemis was morally degrading, with its prostitute-priestesses and pagan practices.

Even today a visitor to Ephesus is awed by the ruins that remain and by what is left of the marble pavement that once formed the streets of that bustling, ancient city.

It was to this throbbing and thriving city that Paul now came. And it was here that he spent three important years of his life. But let's pick up on the drama now as Luke has given it to us.

Upon Paul's arrival in Ephesus, he makes contact with twelve of the Ephesian Christians, and this brings us to the second illustration in our lesson of incompleteness. Evidently, Paul discerned that something was missing in their lives, and so he asked, "Did you receive the Holy Spirit when you believed?" (19:2, NIV). They immediately responded, "No, we have not even heard that there is a Holy Spirit" (verse 2, NIV). All they were aware of was the baptism of John the Baptist. They had obeyed and believed as far as they knew how. But as Paul explained, that wasn't enough, so now he opened up to them the Good News of the gospel of Jesus Christ. They were anxious to complete their faith, and they believed and were baptized again "in the name of the Lord Jesus" (19:5, NASB). And it was then that the Holy Spirit came upon them with great power (19:6).

From the insights given us here in this part of our lesson we see the importance of being complete in our faith and of helping others to know that same experience. We have learned that in Christ we are saved *from* something—sin—and we are also saved *for* something—righteousness. We are moving from being saved by faith to living by faith. Our viewpoint is shifting from looking backward to the beginning point to looking forward to the full challenges of being a Christian indwelt by the living Lord. And it is then that we move from membership to discipleship—a quality of life and a depth of commitment that comes from experiencing wholeness through Christ in the Christian way of life.

Now these twelve Ephesian men had moved from a process (the baptism of John) to a Person (the Holy Spirit). They had moved from ritual to power and beyond *an* experience to the *ongoing vitality* of *the* experience. And this was made possible for them, and for us, by a continuing relationship with Christ, and that is made possible by the Holy Spirit.

Following his experience with the twelve men who had been followers of John the Baptist, Paul immediately turned his attention to a concentrated teaching and preaching schedule in the synagogue in Ephesus. Few details are given us about this period except Luke writes that after three months a dispute arose among the Jews over his teaching, and Paul had to discontinue his synagogue ministry. But he then moved his headquarters to the school of Tyrannus, a philosopher of considerable note.

Paul's Ministry in Ephesus (19:11–20:1)

Confronting the Counterfeit Spirit: Superstition and False Beliefs

The Christian life is not limited only by the incomplete interpretations of it but also by certain counterfeits, which are either a part of it or are in competition with it. In this next part of our lesson we will look at some of these counterfeits. And we will see from this that frequently within the fellowship of Christians we will come up against spiritual frauds.

The first incident might be titled "Confronting the Counterfeit Spirit" (19:13–20).

Ephesus was a center of superstition and sorcery. And with all the mighty works that Paul did there in the name of Jesus, it was only natural that these works would attract the attention of some of the corrupt troublemakers who were involved in magic-for-profit schemes. Apparently, Sceva and his sons—all renegade Jews—had seen some of Paul's miracles, and they attempted to duplicate them by invoking Jesus's name even though they didn't believe in Him (19:13). The results of this skulduggery were disastrous even though there is a hint of humor in what happened. When the scoundrels commanded an evil spirit to come out of a person, "the evil spirit answered them, 'Jesus I know, and Paul I recognize, but who are you?'" (19:15, ESV). And with that the possessed man attacked Sceva and his sons with such furor that they were hurt and had to run for their lives (19:16).

The exposure of these counterfeits, which so vividly illustrated the difference between sorcery and magic and the miracles performed in Jesus's name, impressed everyone in the city. And Luke tells us that many of them became believers and burned their books of magic and their charms.

What does this rather strange (from our point of view) story have to say to us today? It has a practical application because there are still those who use the language of faith without having been truly transformed by Christ, and those who profess a faith in God but who never act it out in daily living. Like Sceva and his family, some people have experienced or witnessed the disastrous results of trying to call on a power they do not possess. And like their Ephesian predecessors (19:19), people today still exchange their superstitions and false beliefs for the real thing—authentic Christianity. And now, as then, when this exchange takes place, the Word of God grows mightily and prevails (19:20), both in individual lives and in the total witness of the church.

As we turn back to the Scripture lesson now, Luke seems to insert a two-verse parenthesis (19:21–22) in his description of these Ephesian events. Although Paul had a passionate concern for the people of Ephesus, his mind was already looking ahead to Greece and Jerusalem—and even to Rome. He had long wanted to personally visit the Imperial City. For years he had traveled the Roman roads in Asia Minor and Greece, now he longed to see the terminus of those roads and preach the gospel there! But it wasn't the Lord's time for Paul to leave, so he sent two representatives to Greece while he remained in Ephesus.

Confronting the Counterfeit Spirits: Idols

We come now to the second confrontation in this part of our lesson (19:24–41). It can be titled "Confronting the Counterfeit Spirits"—plural. The wrong use of the name of Jesus was not the only problem confronting the church in Ephesus. There was a counterfeiting of religion through the production of idols designed by Ephesian craftsmen. But as a result of Paul's preaching, the demand for the silver shrines of Diana was diminishing, and so was the profit for those who made and sold them. And all of this created a crisis between the idol makers and the Christians who were faithful to their Lord.

Luke now introduces a new character, Demetrius, who was not only a spokesman for the "Silversmith Guild" but also a spellbinding orator (19:25–27). He knew that if Christianity flourished, he and his fellow craftsmen would go broke. He had heard the word that wherever Paul went, he insisted that "gods made by human hands are no gods at all" (verse 26, NIV). This was a crisis that had to be met, so Demetrius whipped up the crowd until a full-fledged riot was in the making.

After all, to have their profit-making business disrupted was a serious matter that had to be handled quickly. But there was another issue here that was equally touchy. With clever rhetoric, Demetrius pointed out that if the Christians got the upper hand, their image as a city would be downgraded in all of Asia (19:27). There was an "Ephesian Way" that had to be preserved. Jesus challenged that way by undercutting the very foundations of idolatry in Ephesus and all of Asia.

The Showdown at the Amphitheater

Luke gives us a graphic description of the scene provoked by Demetrius's rhetoric. The crowd became angry and began to chant, "Great is Artemis of the Ephesians!" (19:28, NIV). (Artemis is referred to as "Diana" in the King James Version, using the Greek name for the Roman goddess Artemis.) This apparently ignited the emotional furor of the crowd, and they seized Paul's two Greek companions and rushed to the great theater (19:29). It is not unlikely that it was jammed to its capacity of 25,000. Luke indicates that Paul was not in the crowd at the time this was going on, but evidently when he heard what was happening, he wanted to go and speak to them. But both his fellow Christians and "even some of the officials of the province, friends of Paul," persuaded Paul not to appear (19:30–31, NIV).

The crowd that filled the theater was evidently confused about what to do next. In fact, Luke tells us that many of them didn't even know why they were there; they had just seen a crowd and heard the noise and followed. Finally, they picked up again on the chant, "Great is Artemis of the Ephesians!" (19:34, NIV), and continued doing so for the next two hours. There's something hypnotic about a crowd that moves and chants in unison, and apparently the "town clerk" (19:35, ESV) was afraid things would get completely out of control. And as we've already seen, this was something Rome would not put up with, so he pleaded with the crowd to calm down and not resort to violence but to let the normal process of Roman law take its course. Demetrius and his fellow craftsmen could file charges and the tribunal would make its ruling (19:35–41). The voice of authority broke through their agitated state, and the crowd broke up.

On the surface, the meaning for us from this whole event might seem a bit obscure, but there are certain important lessons here for us. There's much about what we might call the "Ephesian Syndrome" that exists in our world today. There is a tendency to keep Jesus in the background if He and His teachings interfere with our comfort and with our profit. It has been said that the hardest thing to convert is our wallet. If a threat of any kind to our gods of materialism comes on the scene, we tend to revolt and rationalize our way out.

And, like the Ephesians, we don't want our image and our way disturbed. We build our national, cultural, and denominational fences so high that not only do we shut others out, but we can't see out ourselves. But this was not the vision Jesus passed along to His disciples, and it was not Paul's vision. The Christian vision is to the whole world. It doesn't shut people out, and it doesn't exploit them. At the same time, we must stand firmly, as did the Ephesian Christians, against the counterfeit "spirits" (KJV), the idols, the alternative gods, that demand our devotion in time and money and threaten our Christian walk. And perhaps above all, we Christians today must carefully guard against attempting to reshape Jesus to fit our situation and the greed that puts profit and gain above all else.

Paul's long stay at Ephesus had now wound down to a close. It had been a time of victory but also a time of stress. Before leaving Ephesus and closing out his three-year ministry, Paul called the disciples together to encourage them (20:1). These Christian friends had come to mean a great deal to him, and they had been through a lot together as they took their stand against the paganism in Ephesus. The love and support of Christian friends is one of our richest treasures.

Confirming the Saints (20:2–20:38)

Exhortation and Encouragement in Greece

We pick up momentum now as Paul moves out on the final leg of this third missionary journey. We're told that his route took him to Macedonia, where he undoubtedly ministered to the churches in Philippi, Thessalonica, and Berea. And from there he evidently traveled south to Achaia, probably spending most of his time in Corinth.

Throughout Paul's brief visit with the Christians in Greece, his ministry had been one of exhortation and encouragement (20:2). But he was headed toward Jerusalem now. However, just as he was about to take a boat bound for Syria, a plot against his life was exposed, and instead he headed back north from Corinth, overland, to Macedonia, where he and a deputation from the churches there sailed from Neapolis to Troas (20:3–4). And here he continued the ministry of encouragement and confirmation that had marked his visit in Greece. At this stage of its development, encouragement and confirmation were vital for the future of the Christian community in the Graeco-Roman world. Let's watch now the method Paul used in extending this part of his ministry as he moved toward Jerusalem.

The Eutychus Miracle in Troas

First, we see *confirmation through power* in the incident involving Eutychus (20:7–12). The Christians at Troas had come together for worship and to hear Paul. The communion service and the sermon were long. Perhaps in an effort to stay awake, young Eutychus positioned himself in an open window on "the third floor" (NASB), a position from which he might have hoped the breeze off the Aegean would keep him awake. But after a time he dozed off and fell to the ground below and was pronounced dead. But Luke then assures us that Paul took charge of things: "Paul went down and bent over him, and taking him in his arms, said, 'Do not be alarmed, for his life is in him'" (20:10, ESV). What at first seemed to be an unnecessary tragedy was turned into another opportunity to glorify God and confirm the power of the gospel as Eutychus's life was restored to him.

Confirmation through power is still a necessary ingredient in the strengthening of Christians. We might wonder, Why don't we see miracles happening today like they did in the time of Paul? On the surface this seems like a hard question to answer. But when we stop to really think about it on a deep level, we are reminded that God is at work in a miraculous way even in our world today. People are still being touched by the power of the gospel and are being healed physically, emotionally, and spiritually. And this is happening wherever cold and formalized religion is replaced by the warm spirit of the Early Church.

This is not to say that we should try to manufacture miracles. Our faith should not be based on whether or not miracles, by our definition, occur. Jesus warned against that. Rather, our faith should have its roots in the kind of dynamism that says to people, "There's something powerful, transforming, and life-changing about Christianity." May it be said of us as it was of the disciples in Thessalonica, "[They] have turned the world upside down" (Acts 17:6, ESV).

The Stopover at Miletus

Next, we see that Paul brought about *confirmation through proclamation.* Paul was on the move again as he traveled from Troas to Miletus. Here he wanted a last visit with the elders of the Ephesian church, so he sent word and asked them to join him (20:17–35). In this farewell proclamation, Paul stressed the importance of spiritual growth. The key verse in the speech is verse 32: "And now I entrust you to God and to the word of His grace, which is able to build *you* up and to give *you* the inheritance among all those who are sanctified" (NASB).

But let's look more closely now at this part of our lesson, for in it we see certain important ingredients of confirmation. Paul begins by referring to the credibility and integrity of his own life (20:18–20). He reminds the Ephesian elders of his faithfulness to God. In doing this he wasn't giving vent to egotism or self-centeredness. Rather, he was stating the simple fact that words and actions must go together. There can be no greater encouragement than to see God at work in the life of a fellow Christian. And in verse 21 Paul tells them, and us, that it is "repentance toward God and of faith in our Lord Jesus Christ" (ESV) that makes that quality of life possible. In other words, exemplary living is made possible through extravagant grace.

Next, Paul reminds his Ephesian friends that adversity awaits him and all who follow in the way of Christ (20:23–29). Paul was moving confidently toward Jerusalem even though he knew that trouble and affliction awaited him. Verse 24 is a powerful testimony of the work of God in Paul's life: "But I do not account my life of any value nor as precious to myself, if only I may finish my course and the ministry that I received from the Lord Jesus, to testify to the gospel of the grace of God" (ESV). What a marvelous benediction as he tells these friends that he probably will never see them again. But his words were more than a benediction. He knew they would face hard times, even as we do. The Bible gives us no assurance that the payoff for the Christian is a trouble-free life, but we do have the assurance that God's grace is equal to every part of life.

Certainly, this witness of Paul's is important for us today. There is a sort of "prosperity theology" going around that seems to encourage Christians to believe the illusion that God verifies the reality of faith by guaranteeing wealth, health, and other forms of material gain. And the reverse side of that coin says that if we are not enjoying these "blessings," it is a sign of insufficient faith. But this goes against everything that Paul has taught us and what he says here, as well as what we witness in his experiences in the book of Acts.

Paul moved next to urge the Ephesian elders toward a high quality of leadership (20:28–32). The words "Keep watch over yourselves" and "Be shepherds of the church of God" in verse 28 (NIV) are significant. They and we are called to a life of watchfulness—we are to be sensitive to the subtleties of temptation. And the words "Be shepherds of the church" speak of the need to nurture people—one another—in the Lord. We are to build one another up and encourage one another. This attitude is the direct opposite of so much that we see. There is no room for infighting in an atmosphere of encouragement and love.

Paul isn't home yet from this third missionary journey—that comes in the next lesson—but throughout this trip, he has given us a powerful example of what it means to live and witness for Christ. Now in verse 36 we have the third aspect of Paul's ministry: the *confirmation of prayer.* He is telling us that prayer is the lifeline of faith and strength. Prayer has sustained his life, it has empowered him for service, and it has strengthened him in times of suffering.

From Paul we learn that our words are important, our actions are important, but it is prayer that makes our witness truly effective. It is helpful to remember this in our action-oriented society today.

Paul knew that the best antidote to Christian burnout was prayer. Without prayer, we soon discover that we're just going through the motions—we respond and act out of habit. Like Samson in the Old Testament, the power has departed from us and we don't even know it (Judges 16:20).

By Paul's words and actions in this closing scene, his Ephesian friends knew that prayer was the final and ultimate means of confirmation.

For us, the real purpose of prayer is not to get *things* but to get *strength.*

Father, thank You for the strength and grace You give me. Your powerful Word guides, instructs, and nurtures me. Amen.

INSPIRATION FROM THE BOOK OF ACTS

One night the Lord spoke to Paul in a vision: "Do not be afraid; keep on speaking, do not be silent. For I am with you, and no one is going to attack and harm you, because I have many people in this city."

—Acts 18:9–10, NIV

Danger followed Paul like a hunter stalking prey. He could have opted to appease his abusive enemies with silence, never sharing the Good News of Jesus. But Paul refused to choose the easy way out. When he experienced trouble in the city of Corinth on one of his missionary journeys, Jesus appeared to him in a dream, encouraging him and assuring him of His protection. Jesus told Paul he would not work alone. He had prepared those ahead: "many people in this city" who would lend their support and keep Paul safe.

And He did. Paul stayed in that city a year and a half, enlarging his audience to include Gentiles. Just as for Paul and all believers, Jesus prepares His "angels" on earth—not just heavenly ones—to help protect us. We don't need to fear those who might oppose our efforts—sharing about Jesus, the One we represent. The message is so strong, and Jesus is so faithful, that we are covered.

That doesn't mean we won't suffer for the cause of Christ. In His lifetime Paul experienced shipwreck, stoning, hunger, imprisonment, and eventually death. But Jesus kept providing both heavenly and earthly protection until His work for Paul was finished.

He'll do that for us too. The good news of Jesus is too powerful and too precious for us to keep silent.

—Rebecca Barlow Jordan

Notes

Notes

LESSON 7: ACTS 21:1–26:32

Facing the Enemies

Almighty God, it is difficult to face my enemies. Teach me how to rely on Your strength so that I might be able to do so. AMEN.

The Christian faith does not sidestep the fact that sooner or later we must come face-to-face with enemies. This experience has been described variously as "going into the wilderness," "subjected to temptation," and "the dark night of the soul." Sometimes the enemies have been quite tangible, expressing themselves through intense personal misunderstanding and outright persecution. At other times they go under the names of "burnout," "depression," "disease," and "despair." But whatever their name or form, there will inevitably come a time when we as Christians must face enemies of one kind or another.

This fact has been made very clear in our lessons so far in the book of Acts. But now, as the pace increases, Luke seems to focus in this lesson on the reality of opposition to Christianity as we see the Apostle Paul facing his enemies. Now Paul's opposition moves to center stage, and as we trace his experiences and how he handled them, we will see how, in turn, we are to respond to those who oppose us as we attempt to be faithful to the Lord. In using Acts as something of a manual for maturity and discipleship, we can be thankful to

God that the Holy Spirit inspired Luke to deal with this aspect of faith in considerable detail.

Misguided Spirituality (21:1–16)

At the close of our last lesson, we left Paul in Miletus on the Asian coast of the Aegean Sea as he was telling his Ephesian friends goodbye. It was a moving scene because Paul had said this was probably the last time they would see each other.

From Miletus to Tyre

Now, as we pick up on his travels, Luke tells us that Paul's ship sailed south to an island whose name in English is spelled several ways depending on which translation you are reading from—Cos, Coos, or Kos—then southwest around the northern tip of the island of Rhodes, and to the port city of Patara in Lycia (21:1). And from there he caught another ship that took him on a straight course around the southeastern tip of Cyprus and on to Tyre on the Phoenician coast (21:2–3). The third missionary journey of Paul was now drawing toward a rapid close, for he was only approximately 120 miles from his final destination—Jerusalem.

Paul Urged Not to Go to Jerusalem

It was during the week he spent in Tyre that Paul was confronted by "enemies," but this time they were fellow Christians right out of the household of faith (21:4–6). This was a subtle kind of "enemy" and illustrated the *problem of interpretation*. When Paul met with the Christians at Tyre, "through the Spirit they were telling Paul not to go on to Jerusalem" (21:4, ESV). That is about as clear as it can be, and it appears to have the stamp of the Holy Spirit upon it. If we accept that as it appears on the surface, it would seem that Paul was in error in his determination to travel to Jerusalem. But that isn't the whole picture, and this is why it is so important in our study to make sure everything is taken in context.

On two previous occasions Paul had been instructed and motivated by the Spirit to go to Jerusalem. First in Acts 19:21 and then in Acts 20:22, Paul said, "Bound by the Spirit, I am on my way to Jerusalem" (NASB). Both of these verses in the King James text say "spirit" rather than "Spirit," and the New American Standard Bible renders them as "the Spirit," albeit with a footnote that the correct translation also could be "in his spirit" and "in spirit," respectively. The lowercased translation could seem to imply that his decision to go to Jerusalem was based on human desire or determination (his "spirit") rather than by holy direction (God's Spirit). But this is not the case, and the puzzle is cleared up in later translations where the word in those verses is translated "Spirit" or "Holy Spirit."

Paul had been definitely guided by the Holy Spirit to go to Jerusalem. Now the Christians in Tyre told Paul they had word through the Spirit that he should *not* go to Jerusalem. There seems to be a conflict.

Luke doesn't imply in this story that these sincere Christians hadn't gotten a word from the Lord. They weren't deliberately being deceitful, nor had they failed to hear *something* from the Spirit. But what happened was that they failed to rightly *interpret* what they heard.

The fact that this can happen shouldn't surprise us. I'm sure many of us have experienced times when we've run into opposition from other Christians because of a difference of interpretation. And, of course, we've also seen how sharp and bitter divisions occur among Christians and churches when even well-meaning people interpret things differently. This is an "enemy" even today that is not to be taken lightly.

The important lesson for us in this episode is that in confronting every issue or course in life we need to be sensitive to the counsel and opinion of others, but at the same time we must find our guidance through the direction of the Holy Spirit. Frequently, this saves us from making hasty and wrong decisions.

Paul held steady in Tyre in the face of what seemed to be conflicting guidance because he *knew* he'd had positive guidance from God. Apparently, he was able to do this without offending his Christian friends, who were immensely concerned for his safety. So often we Christians offend each other by the strident manner in which we air our "convictions." But if we've received the assurance of God's Spirit, we can relax and follow gracefully.

This was the way it was with Paul in Tyre. God's repeated faithfulness and confirmation kept him from being shaken from the action that he knew was right. His guidance was not based on prejudice or on a hunch. He had positive word from the Lord, and that made it possible for him to rise above the problem of misinterpretation.

Paul's Visit at Caesarea

After a tender leave-taking at Tyre, Paul and his companions moved just a short distance down the coast to Ptolemais, where they spent a day with Christian friends (21:7), and from there they went on to Caesarea and stayed with Philip and his daughters. It was here that Paul had to face a different kind of "enemy" or problem—*the problem of acceptance* (21:8–15).

After a few days, they were visited by an Old Testament–like prophet from Jerusalem named Agabus. With the use of striking symbolism Agabus predicted what would happen to Paul if he went on to Jerusalem: "He took Paul's belt and bound his own feet and hands and said, 'Thus says the Holy Spirit, "This is how the Jews at Jerusalem will bind the man who owns this belt and deliver him into the hands of the Gentiles"'" (21:11, ESV). That was a positive verification of what Paul seemed to know would happen to him.

Immediately, Paul confronted opposition again: "When we heard this, we and the people there urged him not to go up to Jerusalem" (21:12, ESV). Luke, Paul's traveling companions, and the Christians in Caesarea begged him not to go on. But this opposition was not based on any kind of conflicting guidance. They didn't question his guidance from God. Instead, their opposition was based on a deep love for Paul and their desire not to see him suffer.

We see in this what a beautiful relationship Paul had with his friends and fellow Christians. He knew their motive, and he knew they were wrong because of the word he had received from God. But there is a tenderness in this scene that gives us a model for authentic Christian fellowship. Those Christians in Caesarea loved Paul, and he loved them—he admitted they were breaking his heart by their anguish (21:13). But he held firm to his convictions and insisted that he must go on, and it was only then that his friends could say, "The will of the Lord be done" (21:14, KJV).

This scene is reminiscent of the confrontation between Jesus and Peter at Caesarea Philippi (Matthew 16:21–28). After Jesus had made a clear statement about His divine Sonship, He told His disciples that His relationship with the Father would lead to His eventual death in Jerusalem. Peter immediately spoke out with an emotional response, not based on whether Jesus was right. He just couldn't stand the thought of that happening. "'Never, Lord!' he said. 'This shall never happen to you!'" (Matthew 16:22, NIV). And with that, Jesus had to rebuke His friend.

Again, Paul and Luke and the others were on the move. They were taking the last steps on this eventful third missionary journey of Paul's. South and east they went to Jerusalem, where "when we arrived at Jerusalem, the brothers and sisters received us warmly" (21:17, NIV).

Blind Opposition (21:17–23:22)

We've all heard the saying, "Don't confuse me with the facts; my mind is already made up." At times this is more than a humorous aside; it becomes truth. And in this next part of our lesson we see a different kind of "enemy" that Paul had to face. Now the opposition came from his fellow Jews. And as we move along, we will see a demonstration of blind opposition that refuses to look at the evidence. Paul's actions and responses here are most insightful for us as we have occasion to meet similar people and situations in our own lives. As we have walked and sailed with Paul through these lessons, we've been impressed again and again with his courage. But now, as we trace Paul's actions during his arrest and imprisonment in Jerusalem, we are treated to an almost unparalleled exhibition of courage.

The Beginning of Trouble in Jerusalem

Upon his arrival in Jerusalem, Paul discovered that a large number of converted Jews had received word that he, in his missionary journeys, was telling converts from Judaism to leave the Law of Moses behind (21:20–21). Even though this wasn't true, it was clear to the Christian elders that as long as these people believed this, Paul could have no influence over them. So they asked him to make a gesture of good faith by joining and even sponsoring four Jewish Christians in the rites of purification in the temple. They felt that if he did this, it would prove his faithfulness as a Jew to the Law, and once and for all dispel the false rumors (21:23–26).

Admittedly, this is a difficult episode to understand. It raises several questions: Why hadn't the elders defended Paul and denied the rumors before he even arrived? By agreeing to do what they asked, why did Paul do something he didn't need to? Why didn't the Christian Jews show good faith and accept Paul's actions? These questions have plagued Bible students over the years. The Scripture itself doesn't provide us with complete answers to these questions, but as we reflect on Paul's words and actions throughout his ministry, we can make some likely proposals.

Throughout his travels, Paul had never asked Gentile converts to first pledge allegiance to Jewish customs before he would consider them Christians. This was in keeping with the spirit of the Jerusalem Council (Acts 15). But what about Jewish converts? Here the issue was more complex. In general, we can say that Paul asked them to make a difference between dependency and repudiation. In coming to Christ, they were no longer to depend on keeping the Law as their means of salvation. But they were not asked to repudiate their Jewish roots and customs. By complying with the suggestion of the elders and going through the rites of purification with the four other Christian Jews, Paul was trying to show that he had not completely broken with his Jewish heritage. And at the same time, we know that he was not depending on those customs for his salvation.

How does this apply to us? That's a good question—an important one. We have to cope with the same issue today—distinguishing between dependency and repudiation. Often in the heat of post-conversion faith, we give the impression that repudiation of the past is the only way to find authentic Christianity. In doing this we may cause people out of our past to feel rejected because of a "better than you" attitude. It is terribly easy, especially for new Christians, to give the impression of feeling superior and spiritually exclusive and critical of anyone "outside the club." But if this is our attitude, we shouldn't be the least bit surprised if our witness is ignored.

This certainly isn't to say that there aren't things in our past that should be repudiated as we walk with the Lord, but to totally reject our past and the people in it is a mistake. Paul never did this and neither should we if we want to attract people to the joy and wholeness that come from being a follower of Jesus Christ.

Then, too, cooperative gestures are necessary for Christians if we are to remain winsome and relational. Holier-than-thou types have never made good evangelists. If we are to avoid the automatic turnoff, we must continue to relate to and be congenial with those who have not yet made Christian commitments. Our line of demarcation is not the crowd but Christ. But if we expect others to want what we have, it must be attractive and offer promise of a better life.

Paul Is Arrested

Unfortunately, though, Paul's act of good faith in complying with the wishes of the elders did not work out as planned. Instead, the opposition actually increased (21:27–22:22). While it is possible that most of the Christian Jews were satisfied, all the commotion attracted the attention of the large crowds that had poured into Jerusalem to celebrate Pentecost. And in those crowds were Jews from Asia, possibly from the synagogue in Ephesus, who knew about Paul and were violently opposed to his teaching. In addition to accusing him of turning people against the Law, they falsely charged him with taking a Gentile, Trophimus, into the Temple with him (21:28–29).

The rhetoric of Paul's detractors soon incited a mob spirit. In their bitterness and hatred, they threw Paul out of the temple, slammed the doors behind him, and were "about to kill him" (verse 31, KJV). Luke then tells us that the uproar from the riot was so loud that it attracted the attention of the Roman soldiers in the Fortress of Antonia nearby, and they came rushing out to calm things down (21:30–38).

These events caused Paul to shift to a second strategy in dealing with his opposition: *public testimony*.

As Paul was taken into custody, he made it clear who he was and asked to speak to the crowd (21:39–40). The chief captain, obviously surprised at Paul's knowledge of Greek and that he was from Tarsus, granted his request. And so, standing on the stairway of the fortress, Paul addressed the crowd in their own Hebrew language.

Paul's Public Witness

In this magnificent speech (22:1–21) Paul explained the transformation that had taken place in his own life. But first, he clearly identified himself with Judaism: "I am a Jew" (22:3, NIV). Then he went on to give them details from his background, early training, and his early violent opposition to Christianity (22:1–5).

Next, Paul explained the cause of his amazing change: his encounter with Christ (22:6–11). Here he calmly spelled out all that happened to him on the road to Damascus. It was a factual account of an event that happened—nothing to incite further the opposition of the crowd before him.

The final statements of Paul's speech (22:12–21) connect with Judaism in several ways—a reflection of Paul's diplomacy as he builds his case. His mention of Ananias in verse 12 was significant, for Paul described him as "a devout man according to the law, well spoken of by all the Jews" (ESV) who lived in Damascus. Then he referred to God as the

"God of our fathers" (22:14, ESV), clearly implying that his new experience was rooted in and related to his Jewish faith. His entire speech up to this point had been a dispassionate witness of what God had done for him. He wanted them to hear his message so he avoided, as long as he could, language that would turn them off. But when he reached the place in the story where he had to say, "I will send you far away to the Gentiles" (22:21, NASB), the crowd went wild, and they shouted, "Away with such a man from the earth, for he should not be allowed to live!" (22:22, NASB).

What do we learn from this incident? Perhaps most of all we learn that there may be times when we are called upon to express our beliefs and faith to people who disagree with us. But the model Paul has given us in this speech is very important: The spirit in which we do it is equally important. Witnessing to our faith should not be taken as an opportunity to drive a wedge but to build a bridge. Naturally, our testimony doesn't conceal the truth, but it is to be reasonable and understandable and not given in a spirit of condemnation and censure—if we want to be effective.

Saved from the Frenzy of the Mob

We see now in verses 22 and 23 the frenzy of the mob in Jerusalem that day. The commander of the Roman garrison in the Antonia Fortress intervened and had Paul brought into the castle for interrogation. And as was the practice then, the questioning would be accompanied by scourging to ensure they would get the truth. It was a cruel practice in which a victim was bound and then whipped with leather strips to which were fastened pieces of bone or metal. It was against the law to use this *flagellum* on a Roman citizen.

When Paul's attempt to vindicate himself by action and word failed, he moved to his third strategy: *official appeal* (22:25–29). He used his Roman citizenship to prevent a flogging. Paul did this, not because he feared death, but because his mind was set on getting to Rome, and he didn't want to be disabled in any way.

When Paul informed the centurion that he was a Roman citizen (22:25), the soldier immediately reported this to his captain. Luke then tells us that when the chief captain had verified this fact, he "was afraid" (22:29, KJV) because the law had been broken when they tied Paul up. But then his next move was strange. For a reason that Luke doesn't clarify, the chief captain insisted that the Sanhedrin be called into session, and when they were together, "he brought Paul down and set him before them" (22:30, ESV). This was undoubtedly exactly what Paul was hoping for, and he eagerly seized the opportunity.

Paul's Defense before the Sanhedrin

Paul chose his opening words carefully to put himself on their level by addressing them as "my brothers" (NIV), and he asserted that his conscience was clear before God (23:1). With this bold statement the high priest ordered that he be struck in the mouth because of what was interpreted as blasphemy. Paul knew this humiliating act was uncalled for and even illegal under the circumstances, and he lashed back at the one who gave the order, "God will strike you, you whitewashed wall! You sit there to judge me according to the law, yet you yourself violate the law by commanding that I be struck!" (23:2–3, NIV). Obviously, Paul was angry, but when it was called to his attention that the object of his verbal attack was the high priest, Paul apologized immediately. "I did not know, brothers, that he was the high priest, for it is written, 'You shall not speak evil of a ruler of your people'" (23:5, ESV)—a quotation from Exodus 22:28.

There's a lesson for us in Paul's apology at this point. We, like Paul, must be willing to admit we're wrong any time we exceed the bounds of Christian behavior. There's nothing belittling about an honest confession of failure. The wrong comes when we arrogantly refuse to make a wrong right and thereby compound a mistake.

Next, we see Paul as the skilled technician. He knew the Sanhedrin was made up of two conflicting groups—the Pharisees and the Sadducees—so he identified himself as a Pharisee and the son of a Pharisee (23:6). This threw the council into an uproar because of the opposing positions of the two parties over the subject of the resurrection. At least some of Paul's fellow Pharisees were all for letting him go at this point, but the rest of the crowd created such an uproar that the Roman chief captain took him into custody again to save his life (23:7–10). In this scene, Paul proved a point that both frustrated and infuriated his enemies: if they couldn't agree among themselves about the interpretation of the law, on what grounds could they accuse him of being unfaithful to it?

We also learn from this scene that there may be times when we, in faithfulness to our Christian witness, may need to use official appeal. Our stand against evil in any form may take us before both political and legal authorities, and when it does, we find a model in Paul of integrity and responsibility.

Luke now tells us that Paul's reward came as assurance from the Lord that his dream would come true: "Take courage! As you have testified about me in Jerusalem, so you must also testify in Rome" (23:11, NIV). This was a promise Paul would have cause to lean upon many times in the months and years ahead.

The Plot to Kill Paul

But the plot against Paul thickens as Luke tells us how more than forty men banded together and swore to kill the apostle. "We have strictly bound ourselves by an oath to taste no food till we have killed Paul" (23:12–15, ESV). This was not a threat to be taken lightly. The conspirators were deadly serious as they devised their plot.

Fortunately, though, through an undisclosed means, Paul's nephew heard about the plot and was able to get to his uncle and warn him. Paul, in turn, sent the young man to the chief captain, where he exposed the details of the plot. Paul had recognized the seriousness of what was about to happen. He knew his life was in jeopardy, so he took the one course of action that was open to him—to seek *personal protection*. He knew there was no way he could protect himself, so he had his nephew act in his behalf (23:17–21).

Paul Escorted to Caesarea

Now we get a vivid picture of just how dangerous this situation was. The chief captain to whom Paul's nephew reported had to be a seasoned Roman soldier with wide experience.

He recognized the danger and took steps to move Paul out of Jerusalem to Caesarea, the seat of the Roman government in Palestine. But look at the precautions he took. The escort party was made up of 200 soldiers, 70 horsemen, and 200 spearmen—a total of 470 men. That's a lot of security to protect one prisoner! But this hardened soldier knew what he was up against, and he wasn't taking any chances. As soon as he composed his official letter to Governor Felix, the procession took off under cover of darkness, traveled the 60 miles to Caesarea, and the delivery of the prisoner was made successfully and without incident. Paul was now a prisoner in Herod's palace.

We see in this story that Paul knew his life was important—God had assured him of his worth even as He had assured him he would "testify in Rome also" (Acts 23:11, NASB). Paul was willing to risk much for the sake of the gospel, but he never did it with the attitude that "my life doesn't matter." The whole point of this final drama is that his life *did* matter! And when it became clear that he was in danger, he took the necessary steps to protect himself.

From these experiences of Paul's we are reminded again that *we* are important to God. Our welfare and our lives are significant in His plan. While most of us don't face physical danger because of our faith, we are at times exposed to social, vocational, and even spiritual pressures that are crippling and possibly a serious threat to our emotional health. In such times of stress, we can be certain that God cares. But at the same time we, like Paul, are to use all the means at our disposal to protect ourselves against those people and forces that seem determined to defeat us. This is fully consistent with Christian discipleship.

Expedient Neutrality (24, 25, 26)

Most of us have probably had a situation in our relationships with other people that is sometimes referred to as being "stonewalled." This simply means that the other party (often someone with an opposing viewpoint or goal) gives every appearance of being open and interested, but in reality that is nothing more than a ruse, because that openness is never acted upon. This is a terribly frustrating way to be treated, and it can frequently be recognized when the other person says such things as "I hear you" or "We'll certainly look into that." But that's the end of it because nothing ever happens. You could call it the way of expedient neutrality.

Chapters 24, 25, and 26 of Acts show this phenomenon at work in Paul's life. The events in these chapters occurred over a span of two years, probably AD 58 to 60. Paul remained in prison in Caesarea throughout this time. During his incarceration, he made three dramatic appearances before the authorities. And each time we see that he was being stonewalled—a victim of expedient neutrality. But Paul handled each of the three appearances with a forthrightness and decorum that underscored his genius and left with us a model for Christian action when we receive similar treatment.

Paul's Trial before Governor Felix

Paul's first trial opened just five days after his imprisonment at Caesarea. A contingent of the Jewish elders headed by Ananias, the high priest, traveled from Jerusalem to lay their charges against Paul before Felix, the Roman governor. The prosecuting attorney for the Jewish hierarchy was a glib lawyer named Tertullus, who opened his arguments with a layer of flattery aimed at Felix that was calculated to make a favorable impression (24:1–4).

Before going ahead, though, let's look a little closer at Governor Felix. He succeeded Pilate as governor and was every bit as incompetent as his predecessor. He likely obtained his appointment simply because his brother was a good friend of Emperor Nero. His administration was marked by gross irregularities that were exceeded only by his infamous character. He had been married twice before marrying a Jewess named Drusilla, one of the daughters of King Agrippa I. Tacitus, the Roman historian, described Felix as "a master of cruelty and lust, who exercised the powers of a king in the spirit of a slave." Because of his disgraceful and incompetent administration, Nero finally recalled him around AD 58.

This was the man before whom Paul appeared in his first trial, and as the events unfold now, we will see an example of *knowledgeable indifference* (24:1–27). After his fawning introduction, Tertullus spelled out the charges against Paul: (1) He was a pesky troublemaker; (2) he was the ringleader in the Nazarene sect; and, (3) he had defiled the Temple (24:5–6). He then condemned Lysias, the chief captain, for taking Paul out of their custody "with great violence" (24:7, KJV). The clever prosecutor built his case on false charges and half-truths.

At a signal from the governor, Paul gave a brilliant response to the charges (24:10–21). It is not the purpose of this particular lesson to replay the fine points in detail of either the prosecutor's charges or Paul's defense because it will be to our benefit to keep our attention focused on Governor Felix.

Perhaps the most intriguing thing Luke tells us about Felix is that he was very familiar with "the Way"—a term for the Christian movement at that time (24:22). And now Paul had evidently made a strong impression on the governor because after Paul made his defense, Felix adjourned the court for a few days in order to give Lysias the opportunity to appear (24:22).

Some days after that, Felix, accompanied by his wife, Drusilla, "sent for Paul and heard him speak about faith in Christ Jesus" (24:24, ESV). It may be that Felix wanted merely to show off his prisoner before his young wife. But Paul's witness to the power of the Christian gospel was so strong that Luke says "Felix became frightened" (verse 25, NASB). Actually, the Greek word used here is much stronger than what most English translations suggest, and it implies that the governor was struck with terror.

This is understandable because Paul spoke of the need for righteousness and self-control and of the coming judgment. All of this seems to have moved Felix deeply but not to the point that he was willing to accept Christ. In fact, Luke goes on to tell us that there were several such confrontations later, but apparently he felt the governor's sole purpose was in the hope that Paul would try to purchase his release (24:25–26). Instead, Paul was kept in prison for two years, and Felix comes down to us as an example of how a person can be knowledgeably indifferent.

Perhaps you have known people like Felix, who know (or think they know) just a little bit about Christianity—but not enough to have really experienced it. This kind of person tends to be either hostile or—like Felix—indifferent. Either way, we, like Paul, are to be faithful to our witness in words and actions and leave the results to God.

Paul's Trial before Governor Festus

The action in the Acts story picks up again. Felix is recalled and is replaced as governor by Porcius Festus. Among the unfinished business Festus inherited was the disposition of Paul's case. In a series of fast-moving verses (25:1–8), we find Paul making his second trial appearance before the authorities. Again the Jewish leaders leveled their old false charges against him. For two years they had been foiled in their efforts to get rid of Paul once and for all. Festus evidently saw that their case was weak, but nevertheless, he was anxious to escape responsibility. Historians such as Josephus paint him as basically a decent man, but he was anxious to win the favor of the Jewish religious leaders, so he asked Paul if he would be willing to be tried in Jerusalem (25:9). This was a clever dodge on the part of Festus, but Paul knew that to go to Jerusalem would mean certain death.

In the case of Festus, Paul was now having to cope with a different kind of "enemy": *considered detachment*. It was obvious that Festus was trying to find an easy way out. If Paul had agreed to a Jerusalem trial, Festus would have been a sort of "figurehead judge"—a part of the scene, but not really, because they would be in the religious environment in Jerusalem. Paul, however, saw what was happening and made his formal appeal to Caesar. With this action, the future course was set.

Paul would head for Rome, and no doubt Festus was pleased because this took him out of the picture (25:10–12).

With Festus, we see what can happen when a person is well-intentioned but unwilling to become involved. Whenever someone says, "Do whatever you have to do; just leave me out of it," we are confronted by an "enemy" of detachment. When we really care about a person or situation, *we become involved.*

Paul's Trial before King Agrippa

The final act in this drama brings Paul face-to-face with King Agrippa, who, as we shall see, came to represent the "enemy" characterized by *interested activity.* Agrippa was a relatively unimportant king who ruled over a small piece of Palestinian territory. He moves into the scene now along with his wife, Bernice, to pay his respects to the new Roman governor. Festus apparently knew that Agrippa was very familiar with the Jewish religion, so we find him explaining Paul's case to the visiting king (25:13–22). And next we learn that Agrippa was so interested that he said, "I would also hear the man myself" (25:22, KJV). And now we move into one of the most interesting stories in the book of Acts.

Historical information would give us cause to believe that Agrippa's desire to hear Paul was based on more than just a fulfillment of duty. He was a grandson of King Herod, who had been told about the birth of Jesus by the wise men and had then ordered the murder of the male children in and around Bethlehem. His father, Agrippa I, had executed James and imprisoned Peter. The tragic death of Agrippa I is described in Acts 12:20–23. When Agrippa II appears on the scene, we could almost say that animosity for Christianity was in his genes. Nevertheless, he consented to hear Paul out (25:22), although we are not told why he wanted to get involved in the dispute. It is possible that Luke included the incident in such detail in order to make two points.

First, we can never predict how people will react to the gospel. If family line were any indicator, Agrippa would have been placed on the "hopeless" list. It would have been impossible for him to have been reared in the Herodian environment without having heard the stories and seen the anger and hatred in both his father and grandfather. If ever there was a person predisposed to rejecting Christ, it was Agrippa. But as this scene clearly shows, Agrippa was both moved and intrigued by what he heard.

As a young student in his early twenties, Lew Wallace was fiercely opposed to Christianity. He and a friend determined to investigate the Christian phenomenon, especially the person of Christ, with the intent of producing a book that would discredit the whole affair. The story is now history. In the process of researching the person of Christ as portrayed in the Bible, Lew Wallace was converted. Published in 1880, the resulting novel, *Ben-Hur*, promoted a positive view of Christ and Christianity, sold more than 300,000 copies in ten years, and as a work of literature helped to popularize the historical novel as an acceptable literary form. All of this was by one who started out determined to undermine the whole thing!

We must not be too quick to pigeonhole the "Agrippas" in our circle of acquaintances. Where they would seem to be headed may not be where they wind up. It might just be that Agrippa had heard so many bad things about Christianity that he decided there must be something to it or else his father and grandfather would not have spent so much time trying to stamp it out. Like Shakespeare's character in *Hamlet* who said, "The lady doth protest too much, methinks," Agrippa may have sensed in his forebears an overreaction, at least to the extent that he wanted to check it out for himself. We learn from this that it is a mistake to write off anyone as a likely candidate for Christianity.

But the second point is equally important: interest alone is not enough to produce conversion. Agrippa certainly gave Paul an honest hearing as we see in Luke's lengthy account (26:2–29). Because this is one of the longest defenses recorded in Acts, we will look at it more closely in a moment. For now, it is useful because it shows that Agrippa was interested, and even more in what Paul had to say.

We mustn't read more into the king's response to Paul than is intended. His words, rendered here in the familiar words of the King James Version, read as "Almost thou persuadest me to be a Christian" (26:28). This is not accurate in terms of the way we use English today. It implies that Paul came within a hair's breadth of converting the king. In actual fact, the king was moved, but not that much. The Greek term isn't easy to interpret. It allows this kind of an expanded translation of Agrippa's words, "I see what you're up to. You think that in these few words you can persuade me to become a Christian." The Amplified Bible communicates some of Agrippa's ambivalence in verse 28: "In a short time [and with so little effort] you [almost] persuade me to become a Christian," as does the New International Version: "Do you think that in such a short time you can persuade me to be a Christian?" In other words, Agrippa apparently saw that beyond the testimony was Paul's deeper evangelistic intention. And at that point, the king's background took over, quashing any interest that the testimony might have kindled.

In fairness to Agrippa, his assessment of the situation was accurate. Paul had done nothing to deserve death (verse 31). And as far as we can tell, Agrippa found no fundamental fault with the gospel as Paul had presented it. But even interested inactivity on the king's part failed to change anything. Paul went on to Rome, and Agrippa remained an unbeliever. For Agrippa, the expedient thing to do was just to leave things as they were both for himself and for Paul.

Paul's Attitude during His Appearance before King Agrippa

Before leaving this lesson, though, we need to look more closely at Paul's testimony before Agrippa. In it we find several reminders of attitudes and approaches that can help us as we bear witness for our faith.

First and up front, we detect a note of *courtesy* (26:1–3). In our witness for Christ, we must remember that no good can come from any other approach. Whenever we lose respect for another person's humanity and position, we have undermined the opportunity for fruitful interpersonal relations and Christian witness. It's a mark of simple human decency to show respect to another person. Paul knew Agrippa's background, and he saw through the pompous front, but this did not erase the note of courtesy from the introduction to his witness.

Second, we cannot help but be moved by the *content* of Paul's witness. Through a mixture of biography and theology, Paul sought to give the king enough to go on to make a personal decision about the faith. On this occasion, Paul began with himself and ended with Jesus—showing how Christ had led him to embrace an entirely new way of life. Basing his words on Agrippa's supposed authority, the Old Testament, Paul showed how Moses and the prophets would support his experience and testimony. But if Moses and the prophets were too far in the past, he offered himself as a living example of all they had said. This blend of information and experience should always characterize the content of our witness.

Third, Paul gave a clear *challenge*. We've already seen, even as Agrippa himself saw, that Paul's few words were intended to do more than report an experience. Their purpose was to lead Agrippa to a personal experience with Christ as well. The final words in Christian witnessing are not "and that's what happened," but rather "and that's what happened—*now what about you*?" Witnessing without an invitation to commitment is only part of the story.

Most of us are inspired at Christmastime as we participate in the joy of the season. The Nativity scenes, the Christmas trees, the singing of carols, all give expression to our traditional love and acceptance of the Christmas story. But the *story* of Christ is quite different from the *claim* of Christ. It's easy for people to accept the babe in the manger. It's the adult Christ who walks into the landscape of our lives that challenges us to a life-changing commitment. Paul knew that day as he stood before Agrippa, Bernice, and Festus that the mere telling of his story wasn't enough. And so he urged them to share in his experience.

As we read the lines and between the lines of Luke's closing scene in this drama (26:30–32), we catch a hint as to just how profoundly impressed the Roman governor and the king and queen were with Paul. And I'm sure it wasn't just his words that got through to them but also his calm attitude and demeanor. They were impressed!

As we have walked with Paul through this lesson, there has been much to learn. But Luke, in all that he has had to say, helps us to face realistically the fact that we will confront "enemies" of all kinds and degrees in our Christian walk. But in the resurrection of Jesus Christ we receive the ultimate proof that "greater is He who is in you than he who is in the world" (1 John 4:4, NASB). This was the confidence that Paul had as he faced the various enemies in his life. And that is our confidence too. Christ is risen! Christ is alive! Christ is with us!

Father, help me develop resolute conviction like Paul,
give me discernment to communicate my convictions
without being offensive, and let my convictions
be based on Your Word. AMEN.

INSPIRATION FROM THE BOOK OF ACTS

Several days later Felix came with his wife Drusilla, who was Jewish. He sent for Paul and listened to him as he spoke about faith in Christ Jesus. As Paul talked about righteousness, self-control and the judgment to come, Felix was afraid and said, "That's enough for now! You may leave. When I find it convenient, I will send for you."

—Acts 24:24–25, NIV

"Convenient." Felix wanted to hear about Jesus when it was convenient. Those words gave me a cold chill and also convicted me. How often have I put my convenience before Jesus? I'm so grateful that Jesus isn't convenient.

Grace—free and undeserved—isn't convenient when I've been striving to earn God's favor in my own power.

Surrendering to His Lordship isn't convenient when I'm trying to control everything and everyone around me.

A heart of praise and worship isn't convenient when I'm savoring a time of venting and complaining.

I can choose my pitiful and false convenience, or I can let Jesus gloriously interrupt my life, my thoughts, and my heart.

Poor Felix. When he heard about faith in Christ Jesus, he sensed a major shakeup to the status quo. He gave in to his fear and pushed the truth away. I wonder if he ever found a more convenient time to give Jesus room in his life.

—Sharon Hinck

Notes

Notes

LESSON 8: ACTS 27:1–28:31

Faithful to the End: Paul's Journey to Rome

Loving Lord, thank You for Your faithfulness. Amen.

In many of the devotional classics, life is described as a journey. Spiritual growth is seen as a pilgrimage in which we increasingly mature in the faith. In our journey, though, we frequently come up against unexpected events and trying circumstances that severely test our commitment. But faithfulness throughout the entire journey of life is the ultimate mark of a person devoted to Jesus Christ.

As we move now into the last lesson of this adventure-packed book of Acts, we follow closely in Paul's footsteps and observe his faithfulness as Luke takes us toward the end of the story.

Making It through the Storm (27:1–44)

Paul had long dreamed of seeing Rome, of taking his witness for Christ to the Eternal City. Luke now prepares us for the fulfillment of that dream. "And when it was decided that we should sail for Italy, they delivered Paul and some other prisoners to a centurion of the Augustan Cohort named Julius"

(27:1, ESV). Three ships and more than 1,000 miles would be involved in this long and hard trip. And early in the journey Luke writes ominously that the "winds were contrary" (27:4, KJV). This was true throughout much of the trip. As we move ahead now through the events of this twenty-seventh chapter of Acts, we will discover insights that can help us make it through the storms in our lives.

From Caesarea to Sidon—an Experience in Friendship

When the ship sailed north from Caesarea, Paul must have felt a tremendous thrill. Even though he was a prisoner, he was accompanied by two of his closest friends and was headed for Rome. Luke, the "Beloved Physician" and writer of this story, was with him. And the second friend was Aristarchus, one of Paul's converts in Thessalonica. Both of these friends were long-time traveling companions of Paul. Mention is made of one or both of them in Colossians 4:10 and 4:14, in 2 Timothy 4:11, and in Philemon 24.

Frequently, God works through Christian friends to provide support and encouragement during difficult times. You've probably heard someone say—or perhaps you yourself have said—"If it hadn't been for _____, I couldn't have made it." That's true! When our strength and faith are weak, we can draw on the strength and faith of others. Being a friend and having friends is important in the Christian community. This is one of the reasons Jesus surrounded Himself with His disciples. And when He sent them out on a special mission, He arranged for them to travel in pairs. We draw support from one another.

Within a day or so the ship put into port at Sidon, just a short distance up the coast, and it was here we see that at times friendship can come from unexpected sources. Here Luke gives us a hint of what was undoubtedly the beginning of an unusual relationship when he writes, "Julius, in kindness to Paul, allowed him to go to his friends so they might provide for his needs" (27:3, NIV). In other words, Julius allowed Paul to leave the ship at Sidon and visit with some Christian friends there. Then, as we move along through the rest of this journey with Paul, we see a unique and friendly relationship develop between jailer and prisoner. Julius was respectful and courteous to the apostle, and finally, when he turned Paul over to the authorities in Rome, he seems to have arranged for a continuation of that same kind of treatment (28:16).

We never know where help and gestures of friendship may come from.

Paul must have had the great gift of *being* a friend and of receiving the blessings of friendship. As Christians, we are to be known by our acts of love. Sometimes being friendly is our strongest witness of Christ's presence in our lives.

From Sidon to Crete

After leaving Sidon, the ship moved north following the coastline, then turned west between the island of Cyprus and the mainland of Asia Minor. It was here that they first encountered trouble "because the winds were against us" (27:4, NIV). Staying close to the coastline helped them make headway against the west wind that prevailed at that time of the year and docked at the Lycian port city of Myra.

Myra was an important port of call for both Syrian and Alexandrian ships. And Luke tells us now that Paul and all of the prisoners were transferred to a grain ship from Alexandria that was headed for Italy. Then after leaving Myra, the ship moved on west against the wind for another 200 miles or so and put in at Cnidus on the far western tip of Asia Minor.

Because of the contrary winds, when they left Cnidus, instead of sailing due west to Italy, they cut south to Salmone on Crete and continued on the south side of the island to a place called Fair Havens, which was near the town of Lasea (27:7–8). And it was here that we see how Paul used good *common sense* to help him confront another problem or "storm" in his life.

Luke drops a very significant statement in the ninth verse when he says, "The fast was now already past" (KJV). This is a reference to the Day of Atonement that was celebrated between late September and early October. In AD 59, the most likely year of this trip, it fell on October 5. It was a dangerous time of year to be traveling on the Mediterranean. Paul knew this from his earlier missionary journeys, and he urged them not to go on against the adverse weather conditions and warned that harm could well come to both the ship and passengers (27:9–10). But Paul's common sense did not prevail against the will of the centurion and the ship's captain, who wanted to sail on west some 60 miles to the harbor at Phoenix (called Phenice in the King James Version). They didn't take Paul's advice, but that didn't change the rightness of his judgment, as we shall see.

Before going on to the next part of the journey, we should take a moment to examine a point that is quite important, even though it's a bit obscure. When Paul warned the centurion and the ship's master against going on, he indicated that to do so would result in tragedy and loss of life. As we shall soon see, he was only partially correct. And so we can ask ourselves, "Does this mean that Paul, in this case, should not have relied on his judgment and common sense?" No, it illustrates the truth that as we move along at each stage of our life, we must "walk in the light that we have at that moment" and trust God for the results. We'll have an illustration of this happening in the next part of the story.

Caught in the Storm

As the ship was preparing to leave Fair Havens for their winter port of Phoenix, the sailors were encouraged by the presence of a gentle south wind. With this good sign, they cast off, but shortly "a tempestuous wind, called the northeaster, struck down from the land" (verse 14, ESV). This wild northeast wind drove them out to sea and threatened to carry them clear across the Mediterranean to the Sytris banks, a notorious graveyard for ships, located off the coast of Africa west of Cyrene (27:13–26).

The crew and passengers were terrorized by the violence of the storm, and they gave up any hope of being saved (27:20). But now we see a calm Paul drawing on the *resources of his faith* as he confronted this new crisis. And we see him, a prisoner, rising to the place of leadership. In the twelfth verse they had refused his advice; now they accepted it.

The crew had lightened the ship and trimmed the sail, but the ship still drifted on in the storm. In the midst of this seemingly hopeless situation, though, Paul gave them the good news that came to him from an angel of God who said, "'Do not be afraid, Paul. You must stand trial before Caesar; and God has graciously given you the lives of all who sail with you.' So keep up your courage, men, for I have faith in God that it will happen just as he told me" (27:23–25, NIV).

Paul's faith was rooted in a sure word from God. You might be familiar with the story of Dietrich Bonhoeffer, the German Christian pastor who was imprisoned and executed by Hitler for his faith. Despite the cruel conditions and feelings of hopelessness, Bonhoeffer's faith was an encouragement to his fellow prisoners. On the day of his execution, he reminded them that the end of life here on earth is not the end of the story. His biographer writes that even the hardened Nazi guards were affected by his testimony of faith.

When our confidence is fixed firmly in God's Word, we can "be of good cheer" irrespective of the turn of events. This is the kind of faith that Paul had on that ship in the middle of the storm. And it is this kind of faith that can be ours as we draw on the resources of God in facing the storms in our lives.

A fourth element of making it through the storm is *simplicity*: getting rid of anything that isn't really important and getting down to the basics. The ship's crew had already started to do that in verses 18–19, but they redoubled their efforts as the storm intensified and continued to batter the ship. Now, in 27:27–44 this kind of simplicity is expressed in a further lightening of the ship and in doing those things that are a natural part of life. Both were necessary for survival.

Paul's Fourth Shipwreck

After fourteen days in the storm, the sailors sensed they were near land. In all probability they heard the beating of the surf against the shore. They verified their proximity to shore by taking soundings, and since it was night they threw out four sea anchors and waited for daylight (27:27–29). When it got light, the presence of land was obvious, as was the fact that they were in grave danger of being thrown up on the rocks. Earlier, they had jettisoned the nonessentials. Now went the essentials like the lifeboat and the cargo of grain. They were stripped down now to the bare essentials.

Simplicity is a popular virtue today, with magazines and websites that are designed to help us remove the clutter from our lives. But what makes it more than just a fad is that it has been a way of life in authentic Christianity since the beginning. But still most of us wrestle with the problems of an "overloaded life"—overburdened by demands and schedules and commitments. All of this overload seems necessary and important until we're confronted with a life-and-death crisis. Then we're willing to jettison the things that keep us too busy and the things we work so hard to acquire. At such moments it is only life that matters, not acquisitions.

Luke also tells us that while the crew was getting rid of everything they could in order to lighten the ship and make it easier to handle, Paul urged them to take care of such natural activities as eating. The storm had been so bad that they apparently hadn't eaten anything for fourteen days. Paul knew they would need their strength to meet the crisis of the next few hours. And as they ate, Paul spoke prophetically, assuring them of their safety (27:33–36).

Two things stand out in this part of the story that relate to Christian discipleship. First, we are to be faithful in the stewardship of things and time. We are to simplify life and avoid overloading of any kind. And, second, we are to be faithful in the stewardship of our bodies. On the ship that morning, Paul was intensely practical when he urged the crew and his fellow passengers to get the nourishment they needed for strength. And in facing the storms in our lives, proper stewardship of things and time and health will enable us to become better disciples of the Lord.

Now we move to the climax of this part of the story—the shipwreck itself. By now the crew and passengers had eaten what they could and jettisoned everything else. After daylight they saw a bay and a beach and a creek, so they cut loose from the anchors, raised the sail, and headed for shore (27:39–40). But partway in, they struck a hidden reef, and the ship began to break apart. Everybody was now on their own. Some swam while others floated to shore on pieces of the ship. "And so it happened that they all were brought safely to land" (27:44, NASB). This was Paul's fourth shipwreck (Paul mentions the other three in 2 Corinthians 11:25)—the climax to more than 600 miles of stormy nightmare from Lasea in Crete to the beach on Malta.

Miracles at Malta (28:1–10)

Neither Paul nor any of those with him on the ship knew where they were until they were on shore. But in this next part of our lesson (28:1–10) we get some interesting insights into how God can use the unexpected. They had not planned to stop at Malta. But this interruption became, for Paul, one of God's serendipities.

Paul's Snakebite

Let's pick up on the story of their Malta visit. The wet and cold shipwrecked victims were welcomed by the people of Malta. A fire was built to warm and dry them, but as Paul was adding wood to the fire, a snake escaped the heat "and fastened on his hand" (28:3, KJV). Seeing this, the superstitious islanders assumed Paul was being punished for some wrongdoing. But when he shook the snake off without any aftereffects, they then thought he was some kind of a god (28:3–6).

A Special Healing Ministry

Next we read about Paul's introduction to Publius, the head man of the island who entertained Paul and his party for three days. During that time, Paul healed Publius's sick father. And with that, Paul launched into a three-month ministry of healing that touched many of the islanders. And while Luke doesn't tell us, it is not too much of a stretch of the imagination to assume that Aristarchus, Luke, and Paul had many lively conversations and spiritual discussions during those months.

But the important thing to understand here is that this unexpected, unplanned stop at Malta was used by God to exhibit His great power through Paul.

This story is a good reminder of just how careful we need to be in our attitude toward apparent interruptions. It is terribly easy to become so focused on the details of day-to-day life that we fail to see people and their needs. Reaching out to people in love and friendship can never be an interruption.

Leslie Weatherhead, the great British preacher, once told a story that puts life's interruptions and unexpected events in a divine perspective. He spoke of God as a rug weaver who sits at the front side of the rug pulling each thread through the fabric. The observer stands on the other side—the back—watching the process. To us, the observer, the rug-in-process appears to be a meaningless hodgepodge of threads and knots. Weatherhead then says that it is only when the process is completed that the Weaver invites us to come and look at the finished process from His perspective. Now we can see the beauty of the pattern He has created.

This is certainly how life seems to us sometimes—filled with dangling threads and unexpected knots. But we can hope that none of the knots or threads of our lives are meaningless to God. Each thread has its purpose in the overall design. This seems to be the attitude Paul had during his days on Malta. He looked for and took advantage of the God-moments that occurred even in a place he never expected God to be.

There's another aspect to Weatherhead's weaver story that we should note. It seems that when a thread unexpectedly "flaws" the carpet, the weaver skillfully integrates it into the overall design so that in the end it contributes to the desired final pattern. What a great word of hope for us! Even when something "flaws" our day or appears to ruin our intended plans, these may be beautifully integrated into the total fabric of our lives.

The Payoff of an Unplanned Visit

It is interesting to note that in Luke's final comments about the Malta visit he gives us a little twist by writing that the very people who started out being an interruption to the trip ended up by being the ones God used to supply the needs of the shipwrecked travelers. Luke says they "honored us in many ways; and when we were ready to sail, they furnished us with the supplies we needed" (28:10, NIV).

"Faithfulness to the end" leads us to the place where we can recognize the presence and activity of God in even the unplanned places and events of our lives.

Ministry at Journey's End (28:11–31)

From Malta to the Italian Mainland

The Rome-bound party headed by Julius, the Roman centurion, now boarded their third ship and headed north. From Malta they put in at Syracuse on the island of Sicily, where they stayed three days, and from there they continued north to Rhegium on the southern tip of Italy. After leaving Rhegium they sailed north and west along the Italian coast to Puteoli on the bay of Naples, where they were met by some Christian friends who invited them to spend a week with them. Apparently, this was acceptable to Julius, so arrangements were made.

It is in this concluding section of our lesson that we become aware of a number of parallel features that marked this part of Paul's journey, and which we need to incorporate into ours.

Paul Ministered to by Friends

First, it was at Puteoli that Paul found a *supportive community*. Paul must have been greatly encouraged by meeting these people when he landed. We aren't told in Acts just how or when the Christian faith made its way to Italy and to Rome. But I'm sure the presence of these Christian brethren was a source of encouragement now to the apostle.

And then Luke tells us that when they left Puteoli and headed north overland toward Rome, they were met on the Appian Way by a group of Roman Christians who had undoubtedly been alerted to Paul's progress, possibly by friends in Philippi. Reference is made in verse 15 to Three Taverns and the Forum or Market (depending on which translation you are reading) of Appius, which was located a little over 40 miles southeast of Rome (28:14–15).

Again, Paul was ministered to by Christian friends. No matter where we go or how long we live we never outgrow our need for a supportive community of Christian friends. We are a part of a marvelous worldwide fellowship in which we give and receive strength to and from each other.

Arrival in Rome

In just a few words Luke tells about Paul being delivered to the authorities in Rome. It seems likely that quite a bond had been formed between Paul and Julius. They had been through a lot together from Caesarea to Rome. Although Paul was Julius's prisoner, he had been given deferential treatment throughout the trip. It would have been impossible for Julius to have spent all of that time with his prisoner without being deeply influenced. We catch a hint of this in Luke's description of the prisoner exchange in Rome, "And when we came into Rome, *Paul was allowed to stay by himself, with the soldier who guarded him*" (28:16, ESV, italics added for emphasis). It would appear from this that while Paul was still a prisoner, he received special concessions. Here again, it seems probable that a recommendation from Julius had something to do with that. Were some strings pulled in Paul's behalf? It is certainly possible.

Paul's Ministry as a Prisoner

Next, we see in verses 17–28 that Paul was involved in *consistent activity*. His actions now are a replay of earlier episodes in his life and ministry. From Luke's chronology it would appear that just three days after his arrival in Rome he called the Jews together and explained what was behind his arrest and trip to Rome (28:17–22). And following that, at an agreed-upon time, Paul gave witness to the gospel of Christ, beginning with the Law and the prophets (28:23). As in the past, he received a mix of responses: some believed and others resisted.

For us, Paul is an unparalleled model of Christian faithfulness. He knew what his mission was and he stayed with it. For approximately thirty years he had been faithful to his calling. He presented Christ to all who would listen—Jews and Gentiles; people of high and low estate. He had plenty of opportunity to be discouraged and even to despair. There were times when he may have been tempted to quit and go home, but he never did. The hardships he suffered are difficult for us to imagine, even as we read Paul's own description of them: "Five times I received from the Jews the forty lashes minus one. Three times I was beaten with rods, once I was pelted with stones, three times I was shipwrecked, I spent a night and a day in the open sea, I have been constantly on the move. I have been in danger from rivers, in danger from bandits, in danger from my fellow Jews, in danger from Gentiles; in danger in the city, in danger in the country, in danger at sea; and in danger from false believers. I have labored and toiled and have often gone without sleep; I have known hunger and thirst and have often gone without food; I have been cold and naked" (2 Corinthians 11:24–27, NIV). Yes, he was ever faithful through the testimony of consistent activity.

The whole of Paul's ministry is marked by a consistent strategy, a consistent content, and a consistent purpose. He was always faithful to his calling regardless of the cost. And he carried this same spirit into his ministry in Rome.

We come now to the closing of our lesson as well as our study of the book of Acts. It has been sheer drama from the beginning to this point. In these last two verses (28:30–31) Luke tells us all we know here of Paul's activity in Rome over a period of two years. It is reminiscent of the equally swift summary of Jesus's life and ministry in John 21:25. We wonder, Why didn't the writers go ahead and tell us the rest of the story? And we find ourselves wishing for more. But if we could ask John or Luke why they ended their books this way, they might well answer, "We've told you enough for you to see the purpose of what we've written, *and* enough for you to live out the implications of all that has happened." And with that, we must be content.

We see in these closing verses a pattern of living that gives us an added understanding of Paul's faithfulness to the Lord. His was *a life well lived*, a life of openness and hospitality. He "welcomed all who came to him" (28:30, ESV). He was the kind of person others liked to be around. In that, he was much like Jesus. This is friendship evangelism at its best.

These verses also tell us that even though he was a prisoner, Paul lived a life of courage. Our Scripture text says that he carried on his work "with all boldness" (verse 31, ESV). No doubt he continued to face opposition. But the fact that he was able to teach "without hindrance" (verse 31, ESV) seems to imply that even his opposition had respect for him.

And a third quality of his life that comes through in these verses is that Paul's actions and message were filled with content. He was busy "preaching the kingdom of God, and teaching those things which concern the Lord Jesus Christ" (verse 31, KJV). His hearers were given a vision of an abundant and eternal life, and they were shown the Person who made that kind of living possible. All of this was made real because it came from the experiences of Paul's own life.

The last thing we see about Paul here is that he was a faithful communicator. He preached and taught. And what is equally important, his hearers *listened*. This means not only that the content of his message was good but also that he was skilled in getting it across. By his life and his style of communicating, people were willing to listen.

How much Christian witness today is not heard and received because of the lives and presentation of the "witnesses," many of whom seem unprepared and even angry? Christians can have a tendency at times to use a kind of "in" language that others don't understand. Neither Jesus nor Paul specialized in the use of religious jargon; instead their message was simple and straightforward.

While Luke doesn't tell us here, Paul was also busy as a communicator in writing during these days in Rome. Elsewhere we learn that it was during this time that he wrote his letters to the Ephesians, the Philippians, and the Colossians. These rich and powerful letters spoke not only to the Christians in those days but to Christians across the world for around 2,000 years.

With the completion of these last two verses, Luke stops. He has fulfilled his purpose in writing. In the first lesson, Luke gave us what we've come to call the Great Commission: Christians are to witness for Christ in Jerusalem, in Judea, in Samaria, and to all the world. Following this commission was the story of Paul's life. For more than thirty years his witness had been clear. He gave it with friendliness and courage. The content of his witness was faithful to the claims of Jesus Christ, Savior and Lord. And his witness—his teaching and preaching—was skillfully and carefully given. Luke has given us a thrilling drama of the establishing of the Christian church and its movement out across the world. And he has given us a manual for effective witnessing and discipleship that we can use in our own lives.

Lord, may the lessons in this study and the example Paul set for sharing Your life-changing gospel guide me in all I do. AMEN.

Notes

Notes

Appendix

Miracles in the Book of Acts

Appropriately also known as The Acts of the Apostles, the book of Acts reports that "many signs and wonders were regularly done among the people by the hands of the apostles" (Acts 5:12, ESV). Indeed, Acts is full of exciting reports of miraculous events that took place in the earliest days of the church. Bible scholars have named nearly thirty separate miracles—more than one per chapter. Here in biblical order are just some of the amazing miracles recorded in the book of Acts.

1) The Holy Spirit arrives (Acts 2:2–6), including tongues of fire and speakers from around the world each hearing the gospel in their own language.
2) Peter heals a man who was born lame (Acts 3:2–11).
3) Stephen, who later became the first Christian martyr, "was doing great wonders and signs among the people" (Acts 6:8, ESV).
4) Philip proclaims the gospel in Samaria, and "the crowds . . . saw the signs that he did. For unclean spirits . . . came out of many who had them, and many who were paralyzed or lame were healed" (Acts 8:6–7, ESV).
5) Saul, who then was persecuting and arresting Christians, encounters Jesus on the road to Damascus (9:3–9), blinding Saul, and then Ananias heals Saul's blindness.

6) Peter heals a man named Aeneas in Lydda, who had been "bedridden for eight years" and paralyzed (Acts 9:32–35, ESV).
7) Peter raises Dorcas (aka Tabitha) from the dead (Acts 9:36–41).
8) Peter, arrested and being held in prison by Herod, is freed by an angel (Acts 12:5–17).
9) The Holy Spirit grants Paul and Barnabas "signs and wonders to be done by their hands" in Iconium (Acts 14:3, ESV).
10) In Lystra, Paul heals "a man sitting who could not use his feet. He was crippled from birth and had never walked. . . . And Paul . . . seeing that he had faith to be made well, said in a loud voice, 'Stand upright on your feet.' And he sprang up and began walking" (Acts 14:8–10, ESV).
11) In Philippi, Paul casts a "spirit of divination" out of a young woman (Acts 16:16–18, ESV).
12) Also in Philippi, Paul and Silas, imprisoned for "disturbing the city," are released when an earthquake occurs "and all the doors were opened, and everyone's bonds were unfastened." Despite this, the prisoners remained, and as a result of Paul and Silas's speaking "the word of the Lord to him," the jailer and "his entire household" believed in God (Acts 16:25–34, ESV).
13) When a young man named Eutychus falls asleep and dies after falling from a third-floor window while listening to Paul preach, Paul raises him from the dead (Acts 20:7–10).
14) After being shipwrecked and arriving in Malta, Paul is bitten in the hand by a viper. "He, however, shook off the

creature into the fire and suffered no harm. [The locals] were waiting for him to swell up or suddenly fall down dead. But when they had waited a long time and saw no misfortune come to him, they changed their minds . . ." (Acts 28:3–6, ESV).

15) Also in Malta, Paul heals a man with dysentery, the father of an official named Publius who had welcomed them to the island and "entertained [them] hospitably for three days" (Acts 28:7–10, ESV). After hearing about this, many of the islanders came to Paul and were healed as well.

The outpouring of the Holy Spirit and His work among the early Christians changed the world forever. Though we might not often hear about miracles like the ones we've studied in the book of Acts, the same Holy Spirit is with us today, working in the world through the church and through men and women of faith, just as He was then.

Paul's First Missionary Journey

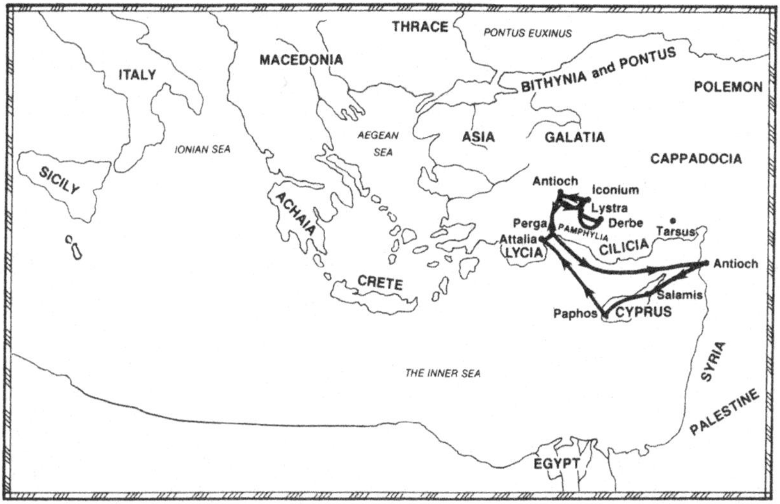

Paul's Second Missionary Journey

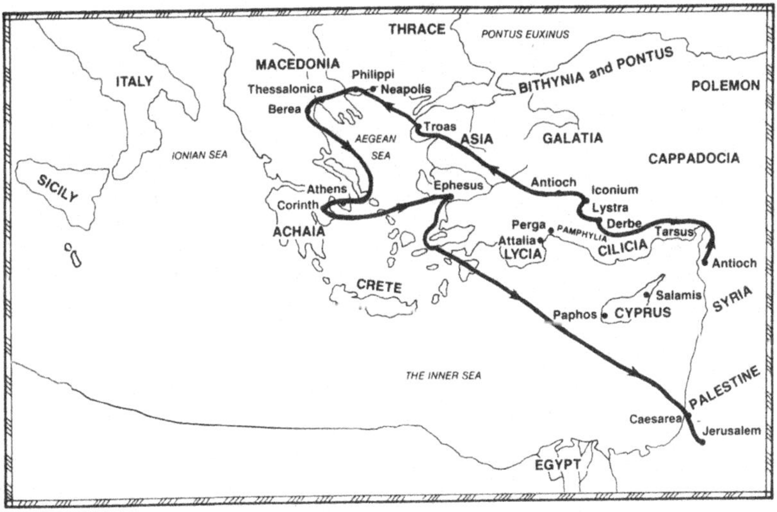

Paul's Third Missionary Journey

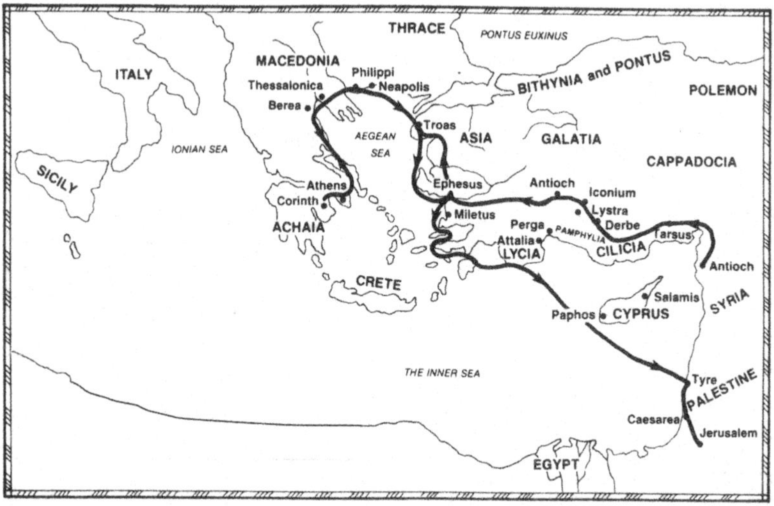

Paul's Journey to Rome

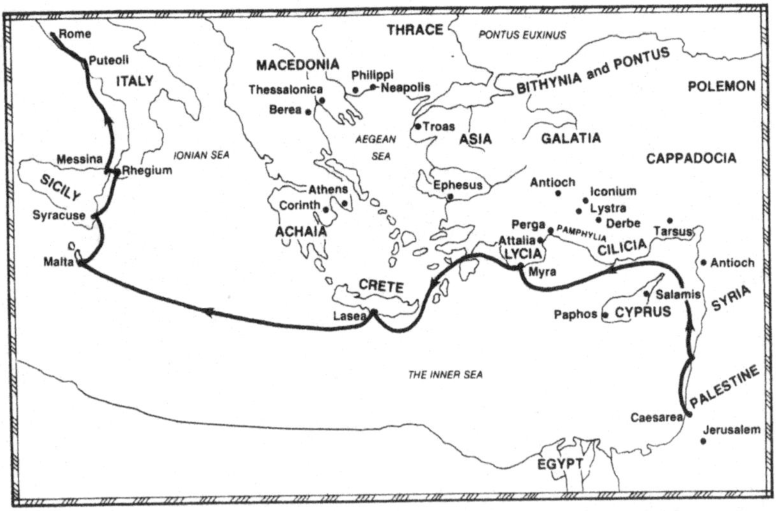

Acknowledgments

A Note from the Editors

We hope you enjoyed *Living with Purpose Bible Study: Acts* published by Guideposts. For over 75 years, Guideposts, a nonprofit organization, has been driven by a vision of a world filled with hope. We aspire to be the voice of a trusted friend, a friend who makes you feel more hopeful and connected.

By making a purchase from Guideposts, you join our community in touching millions of lives, inspiring them to believe that all things are possible through faith, hope, and prayer. Your continued support allows us to provide uplifting resources to those in need. Whether through our communities, websites, apps, or publications, we inspire our audiences, bring them together, and comfort, uplift, entertain, and guide them. Visit us at guideposts.org to learn more.

We would love to hear from you. Write us at Guideposts, P.O. Box 5815, Harlan, Iowa 51593 or call us at (800) 932-2145. Did you love *Living with Purpose Bible Study: Acts*? Leave a review for this product on guideposts.org/shop. Your feedback helps others in our community find relevant products.

Printed in the United States
by Baker & Taylor Publisher Services